Trudi

This Is Music

Books One Through Eight

Senior Author
WILLIAM R. SUR
Michigan State University

ADELINE McCALL
Chapel Hill, North Carolina

BOOKS 1–3

GLADYS PITCHER
Series Consultant

BOOK 4

MARY R. TOLBERT
Ohio State University

BOOKS 1–6

ROBERT E. NYE
University of Oregon

BOOKS 5–8

WILLIAM R. FISHER
State College at Lowell,
Massachusetts

BOOKS 1–6

CHARLOTTE DuBOIS
Series Advisor on Keyboard Experiences
University of Texas

BOOKS 7–8

THIS IS

ALLYN AND BACON, INC.
1962

BOSTON
ROCKLEIGH, N.J.
CHICAGO
ATLANTA
DALLAS
SAN FRANCISCO

ILLUSTRATED BY

DAGMAR WILSON

Music 3

BY

WILLIAM R. SUR

WILLIAM R. FISHER

MARY R. TOLBERT

ADELINE McCALL

Acknowledgments

Grateful acknowledgment is made to the following for permission to use and adapt copyrighted material:

Reprinted by permission of the Association for Childhood Education International, 1200 Fifteenth Street, N.W., Washington 5, D.C. From SONGS CHILDREN LIKE, Copyright 1954 & 1958, "Doing Nothing But Sing" an Old English Rhyme, Alsatian Folk Song, Page 5, and "My Boat" by Ermine and Elsa Cross, Hawaiian Folk Song, Page 42.

For "Christmas Bells Are Ringing" and "Sing a Song of Seasons" from SONGS FOR CHILDREN, copyright Augustana Book Concern, Rock Island, Illinois. Used by permission.

For "Song of the Red Blanket" from NORTH AMERICAN TUNES FOR RHYTHM ORCHESTRA by Gest—Used by permission of copyright owners—Boston Music Company, Boston 16, Mass.

Bureau of American Ethnology for "Lullaby" and "Song of the Peace Pact" from BULLETIN 45.

Richard Chase and The New American Library of World Literature, Inc. for "Old Gray Goose" © 1956 by Richard Chase.

The John Day Company, Inc., publisher, for "Way Out West." Copyright © 1956, 1935 by June Mary Norton and Charlot Byj. Reprinted from SUNFLOWER SONG BOOK by June Norton. Used by permission.

Durand et Cie., Paris, France, Copyright owners: Elkan-Vogel Co., Inc., Philadelphia, Pa., agents, for "Carnival of the Animals." Used by permission.

Sam Fox Publishing Co., Inc. for "The Happy Wanderer" copyright by Bosworth and Co., Ltd., London, for all countries. All rights for the United States of America and Canada assigned to Sam Fox Publishing Company, Inc., New York, N.Y. Arrangements available from Sam Fox Publishing Co., Inc. SA, SSA, SAB, SATB and TTBB choruses; Band; Organ; Accordion. Used by special permission.

Girl Scouts of the U.S.A. for "The Caravan Song" ("Let Us Go Walking"); and "Navaho Happy Song" from the GIRL SCOUT POCKET SONGBOOK, recorded by Marguerite Twohy in New Mexico.

Bradley Kincaid for "I Love My Rooster" from the BRADLEY KINCAID COLLECTION OF FOLK SONGS.

Alfred A. Knopf, Inc. for "Cumberland Gap" from AMERICA SINGS, collected by Carl Carmer. Copyright 1942 by Carl Carmer. Used by permission.

Leeds Music Corporation for PETER AND THE WOLF, Op. 67 by Serge Prokofiev. © Copyright 1956 by Leeds Music Corporation, 322 West 48th Street, New York 36, N.Y. Reprinted by permission. All Rights Reserved.

National Jewish Welfare Board for "Adir Hu" from the JEWISH CENTER SONGSTER edited by Bernard Carp.

The Ronald Press Company and Frederick R. Burton for "Morning Star" from THE RHYTHM OF THE REDMAN by Julia M. Buttree, copyright 1930, renewed 1958.

Union of American Hebrew Congregations for "The Lights of Chanukah" ("The Lights of Hanukkah") by Ray M. Cook from WE CELEBRATE THE JEWISH HOLIDAYS by Rabbi Leonard J. Mervis.

Henry Z. Walck, Inc. for" Hallowe'en Is Very Queer" from SEVENTEEN TO SING, by Gladys L. Adshead and George H. Shapiro; copyright 1946 by Oxford University Press, Inc. Used by permission.

Waterloo Music Company for "Land of the Silver Birch" from FOLK SONGS OF CANADA by Fowke and Johnston; copyright 1954. Used by permission.

Contents

Part I

Time to Sing

MUSIC BY WILLIAM R. FISHER
WORDS BY DORIS R. FISHER

1. It's time to sing, It's time to play,
2. Now we are done, To sing was fun,

1. This is the nic - est time of day;
2. Bring-ing some joy to ev - 'ry - one.

1. When we can sing, When we can play,
2. Of play - ing, too, As you will see,

1. Ev - 'ry - one's hap - py, bright and gay!
2. Soon there'll be more for you and me.

6

PART I

Under Western Skies

Covered Wagons

MUSIC BY RICHARD RANDOLPH
WORDS BY ANNE KAELIN

1. Day aft - er day the wag - ons are roll - ing,
2. Night aft - er night we sit 'round the camp - fire,

1. On - ward and west-ward we ev - er must roam.
2. Sing - ing the songs that re - mind us of home.

Refrain

Roll a - long, roll a - long, cov - ered wag - ons,

Take __ us safe - ly to our __ new home.

3. Some day we'll reach the land of our dreaming,
   Settle and build on some land of our own.
   Refrain

8

Pretend you are strumming a guitar.

Try swaying to this music.

Does the music sway in two's or three's?   (— —) or (— — —)

Can you find a number at the beginning of the song that might tell us?

The top number tells us that there are three counts in each measure.

The bottom number tells us the kind of note which gets one count.

What is the bottom number?

It tells us that a quarter or walking note ♩ gets one count.

The top and bottom numbers together make up what is called a meter signature.

Covered Wagons

(Percussion Score)

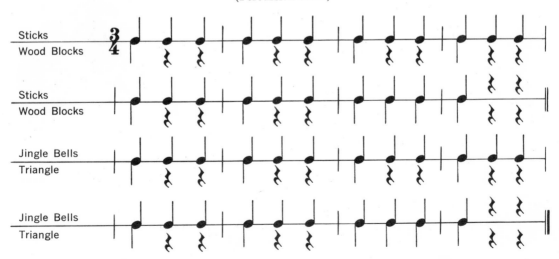

The Old Gray Goose

AMERICAN FOLK SONG

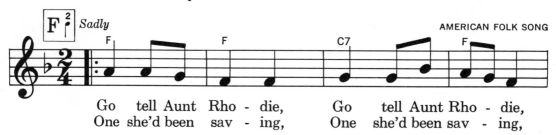

Sadly

Go tell Aunt Rho - die,   Go tell Aunt Rho - die,
One she'd been sav - ing,   One she'd been sav - ing,

Go tell Aunt Rho - die, Her old gray goose is dead.
One she'd been sav - ing To make a feath - er bed.

Repeat

Does this music swing in two's or three's?
What does the meter signature tell us to do?

Keeping a steady beat, try walking around the circle (♩).
Now try running (♫) . Can you do step-bends (♩.) ?
As the inside circle does walking notes (♩) , can the
outside circle do running notes (♫) ?

Try walking and running to these rhythms:

Walk, run, run, walk, run, run, walk, run, run, step-bend.

Run, run, walk, run, run, walk, run, run, walk, step-bend.

As the outside circle moves to one of these rhythms, can the inside
circle move to the other rhythm?

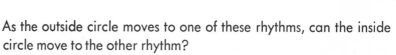

These are repeat signs. They tell us to sing
or play the music between them once more.

Cumberland Gap

1. Lie down, boys, and take a lit - tle nap,

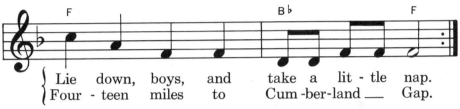

Lie down, boys, and take a lit - tle nap.
Four - teen miles to Cum -ber-land __ Gap.

2. Daniel Boone of Pinnacle __ Rock,
Daniel Boone of Pinnacle __ Rock,
Daniel Boone of Pinnacle __ Rock,
He killed Indians with an old __ flint-lock.

Can you find the meter signature? What does it tell us to do?

Hear the Wagon Wheels

Wag - ons are roll - ing, now hear the wag-on wheels.

Roll-ing on, roll-ing on, wag - on wheels.

Chant the words as you move around the circle.

Move at the same time { *Inside circle:* move to one line of music.
{ *Outside circle:* move to the second line.

Now see if you can make up a tune for each of these lines. The chords
played on the autoharp or piano will help you make up the tune.

I Love My Rooster

AMERICAN FOLK SONG
AS COLLECTED BY BRADLEY KINCAID

1. I love___ my roost - er, My roost - er loves me.
2. I love___ my cow ___, My cow ___ loves me.

1. I love___ my roost - er 'neath the cot - ton-wood tree.
2. { I love___ my cow___ 'neath the cot - ton-wood tree.
    { My lit - tle brown cow___ goes___ moo ___, moo, moo.

1 &2. My lit - tle red roost - er goes cock - a - doo-dle-doo,

1 &2. Dee - doo - dle dee - doo - dle dee - doo - dle dee - doo.

3. I love_my duck_, My duck_loves me.
{ I love_my duck_'neath the cottonwood tree.
{ My little white duck_ goes _quack_, quack, quack.
{ My little brown cow_ goes_moo_, moo, moo.
My little red rooster goes cock-a-doodle-doo,
Dee-doo-dle dee-doo-dle dee-doo-dle dee-doo.

You might like to make up verses of your own using other animals.

The second line of music is sung twice for the second verse and three times for the third verse.

Old Brass Wagon

INDIANA, MISSOURI, AND IOWA
PLAY-PARTY GAME

1. Cir - cle to the left, Old Brass Wag - on,
2. Cir - cle to the right, Old Brass Wag - on,

1. Cir - cle to the left, Old Brass Wag - on,
2. Cir - cle to the right, Old Brass Wag - on,

1. Cir - cle to the left, Old Brass Wag - on,
2. Cir - cle to the right, Old Brass Wag - on,

1. You're the one, my dar - ling.
2. You're the one, my dar - ling.

3. Swing, oh, swing, Old Brass Wagon, . . . (*Link arms with partner and swing.*)

4. Promenade around, Old Brass Wagon, . . . (*In skating position, walk around.*)

5. Sashay up and down, Old Brass Wagon, . . . (*Holding partner's hands, slide in towards the center of the circle and out.*)

6. Break and swing, Old Brass Wagon, . . . (*Drop hands, link arms, and swing.*)

7. Promenade home, Old Brass Wagon, . . . (*In skating position, walk around.*)

As you sing, can you follow the calls to the dance?

13

Oh! Susanna

MUSIC AND WORDS BY STEPHEN FOSTER

1. I — came from Al - a - bam - a with my ban-jo on my knee,
It — rained all day the night I left, the weath-er was so dry,

I'm going to Loui - si - a - na, My Su-san-na for to see.
The sun so hot I froze my-self, Su-san-na don't you cry.

Refrain

Oh! Su - san - na, Oh, don't you cry for me,

For I come from Al - a - bam - a with my ban-jo on my knee.

2. I had a dream the other night, when everything was still,
I thought I saw Susanna dear, a-coming down the hill.
The buckwheat cake was in her mouth, the tear was in her eye,
Says I, "I'm coming from the South; Susanna, don't you cry."

Clap Hands
Tap Heel

etc.

You can dance to this song. Can you make up a dance?

You might like to listen to HOE DOWN from Aaron Copland's *Rodeo*.

14

Oh! Susanna

(Percussion Score)

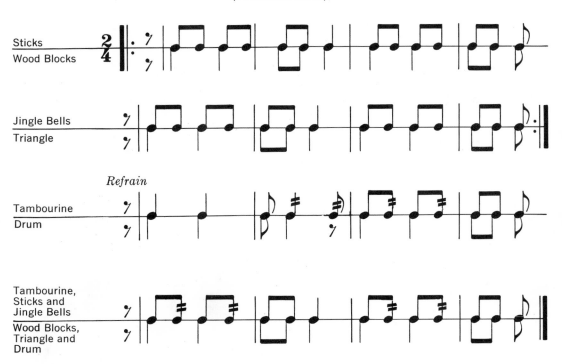

15

Way Out West

MUSIC AND WORDS BY JUNE NORTON

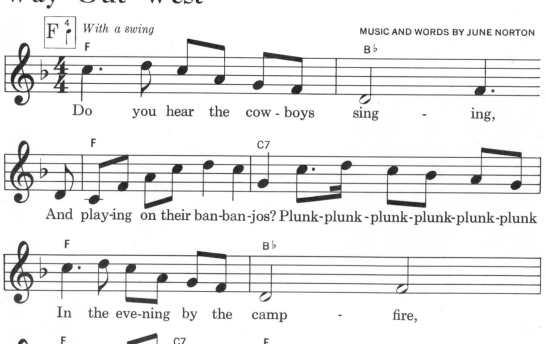

Do you hear the cow-boys sing - ing,

And play-ing on their ban-ban-jos? Plunk-plunk -plunk -plunk-plunk-plunk

In the eve-ning by the camp - fire,

Way out where the cac - tus grows.

Laugh-ing,   danc-ing,   yip-ping, play-ing,

Sing-ing all the songs that ev-'ry   cow-boy knows_____.

Yes,   I hear the cow-boys   sing - ing,

And play-ing on their ban - ban - jos. Plunk! Plunk!
(Bells C   F)

Melodies move up or down by step or by skip.
Find where the melody moves by step.
Where does it move by skip?

Point to the meter signature. What does it tell us?

Pretend you are strumming a banjo.

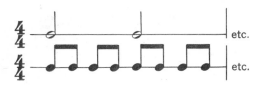

Some of you will want to strum slowly:
Some of you will want to strum quickly:

Home on the Range

AMERICAN COWBOY SONG

1. O give me a home where the buf - fa - lo roam,
2. How of - ten at night, when the heav - ens are bright

1. Where the deer and the an - te - lope play_____ ,
2. With the light from the glit - ter - ing stars_____ ,

1. Where sel - dom is heard a dis - cour - ag - ing word,
2. Have I stood there a - mazed and___ asked as I gazed,

1. And the skies are not cloud - y all day_____ .
2. If their glo - ry ex - ceeds that of ours_____ .

Refrain

Home, home on the range_____,

Where the deer and the an - te - lope play_____,

Where sel - dom is heard a dis - cour - ag-ing word,

And the skies are not cloud - y all day_____.

With your hands show how the melody moves.

C | C | F | G | A

How many times can you find this tune in the song?

The Lone Star Trail

AMERICAN COWBOY SONG

Not too fast

1. I start-ed on the trail on June twen-ty-third,
2. It's cloud-y in the west a - lookin' like _____ rain

1. I been punch-in' Tex-as cat-tle on the Lone Star Trail,
2. And___ my___ old___ slick-er's in the wagon a - gain,

Refrain

Sing-in' ki - yi - yip-i yap-i - yay, yap-i - yay,

Sing-in' ki - yi - yip-i-yap-i-yay _____ !

Melody
Instruments

Sing { D G G G G B
sol do do do do mi
5 1 1 1 1 3 }

MIDDLE
C

D G B

Where in the song do you find this tune?
Can you find others almost like it?
How are they different?

You can imitate horses' hoofbeats with coconut shells or wood blocks, play-ing first on the handle and then on the block. Play four measures alone, then keep on playing as the others sing the song.

20

I Live in Montana

AMERICAN COWBOY SONG
WORDS ADAPTED

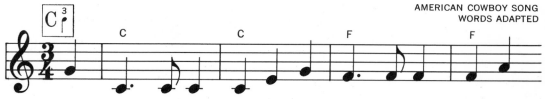

1. I live in Mon-tan-a, you know by my man-ner
2. I live in the sad-dle when round-ing up cat-tle,

1. That I'm a cow-boy, I nev-er will change;
2. I rope and brand them and send them a-long;

1. I love all the plac-es, the wide o-pen spac-es,
2. At night when I lie 'neath the bright star-ry sky____,

1. Wher-e'er the trail leads me while rid-ing the range.
2. I gaze at the camp-fire while sing-ing this song.

Where in the song can you find this tune?

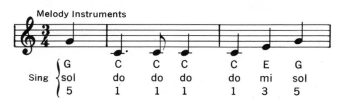

Melody Instruments

Sing	G	C	C	C	C	E	G
	sol	do	do	do	do	mi	sol
	5	1	1	1	1	3	5

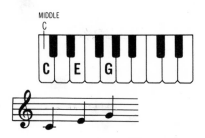

MIDDLE C

21

Leavin' Old Texas

AMERICAN COWBOY SONG

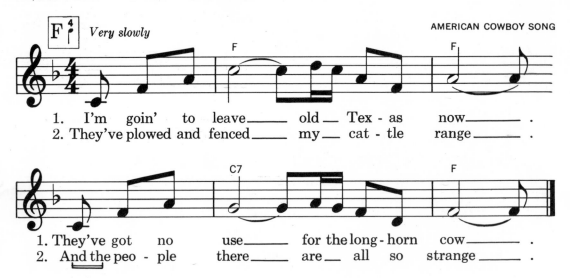

Very slowly

1. I'm goin' to leave____ old _ Tex - as now____ .
2. They've plowed and fenced____ my _ cat - tle range____ .

1. They've got no use____ for the long - horn cow____ .
2. And the peo - ple there____ are _ all so strange____ .

3. I'll take my horse, I'll _ take my rope
   And hit the trail up-on a lope.

4. I'll make my home on the wide, wide range,
   For the people there are _ not so strange.

MIDDLE
C

C F A C

Melody
Instruments

Sing { C F A C
sol do mi sol
5 1 3 5

Some could sing and play these as an
introduction and throughout the song.

Clip clop clip clop clip clop clip clop

Add hoofbeats to the song by play-
ing on coconut shells and tone blocks.

Leav- in' old Tex - as, leav - in' old Tex - as,

22

America's First Music

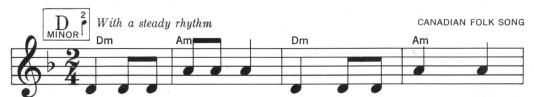

The Indian loves nature. Out-of-doors is so much a part of him that he feels he must sing about its beauty. The Indian sings of trees and forests, animals and birds, sun, moon and stars, mountains and plains, streams and mighty rivers.

Land of the Silver Birch

D MINOR | 2

With a steady rhythm

CANADIAN FOLK SONG

Dm   Am   Dm   Am

1. Land of the sil-ver birch, home of the bea - ver,
2. Down in the for - est, deep in the low - lands,

Gm   Dm   Gm   Dm

1. Where still the might - y moose wan-ders at will
2. My heart cries out for thee, hills of the north.

Refrain   B♭   F   Gm   Dm

Blue lake and rock - y shore, I will re - turn once more.

Dm   Dm   *Becoming softer*

Boom de de boom boom, Boom de de boom boom,

Dm   Dm   Dm   Dm   Dm

Boom de de boom boom, Boo ____ oom ____ .

Play this as an introduction
and throughout the song.

Tom tom $\frac{2}{4}$

Boom   de   de   boom   boom

MIDDLE C

F   A   C D

How many times can you find this in the song?

Melody
Instruments $\frac{2}{4}$

Sing

D	C	D	C	A	F
la	sol	la	sol	mi	do
6	5	6	5	3	1

Does this song sound strange to you? The Indians use a different
kind of scale from ours.

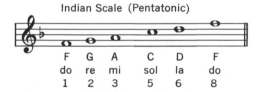

Indian Scale (Pentatonic)

F	G	A	C	D	F
do	re	mi	sol	la	do
1	2	3	5	6	8

Our Major Scale

F	G	A	B♭	C	D	E	F
do	re	mi	fa	sol	la	ti	do
1	2	3	4	5	6	7	8

How many different tones are there in the Indian scale? How many
are there in our major scale? Which tones are left out of the Indian
scale? Which scale is formed by the black keys of the piano?

25

Morning Star

OJIBWAY SONG
WORDS ADAPTED

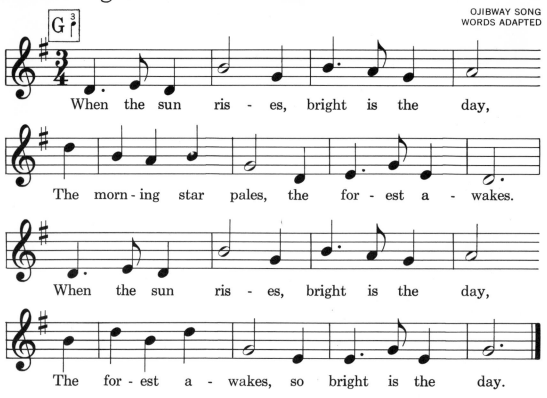

When the sun ris - es, bright is the day,

The morn - ing star pales, the for - est a - wakes.

When the sun ris - es, bright is the day,

The for - est a - wakes, so bright is the day.

Find this in the song and frame it with your fingers. Now play it on melody instruments and sing it.

MIDDLE
C

D E G B

Sing

D	E	D	B	G
sol	la	sol	mi	do
5	6	5	3	1

Tom-tom $\frac{3}{4}$

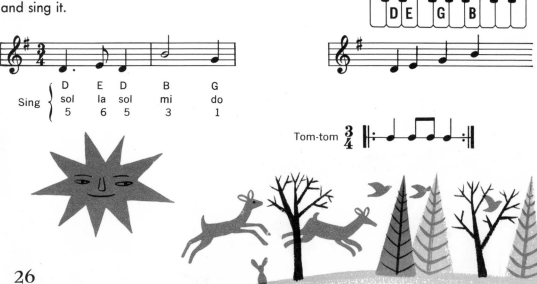

26

Dakota Hymn

UNITED STATES INDIAN SONG
WORDS PARAPHRASED BY
PHILLIP FRAZIER OF THE DAKOTAS

Man - y and great, O God, are Thy things.

Mak - er of earth and sky.

Thy hands have set the heav - ens with stars,

Thy fin - gers spread the moun - tains and plains.

Lo, at Thy word the wa - ters were formed;

Deep seas o - bey Thy voice.

The Indian brave hunts in the forest and fishes in the streams. The squaw tends the fire, cooks the food, and takes care of the little children.

Song of the Red Blanket

ADAPTED OJIBWAY SONG

1. I will go to the for-est deep, I will go to the for-est dark.
2. I will come from the for-est deep, I will come from the for-est dark.

1. I will go to the for - est deep, There to gath-er_ birch-wood bark.
2. I will come from the for - est deep. I will bring the_ birch-wood bark.

Drum and smoke signals were used by the Indians for sending messages from village to village. Can you make up a message and have someone answer it? Play each a number of times.

Where do you find this music in the song?

Melody Instruments

Sing	A	A	A	G	F	G	G	F
	mi	mi	mi	re	do	re	re	do
	3	3	3	2	1	2	2	1

Here is one to be played on a drum.

Message

We have found a bear in the for - est.

Answer

We will help you catch him, we will help you catch him.

Lullaby

ADAPTED CHIPPEWA TUNE
WORDS BY DORIS R. FISHER

1. Sleep my lit - tle one _____ .
2. Hush my lit - tle one _____ :
3. Way,* way, way, way, way _____ ,

1. Now the sun has gone to rest _____ ,
2. For - est friends are sleep - ing now _____ ,
3. Way, way, way, way, way, way, way _____ ,

1. In the soft twi - light all is still _____ .
2. Close your dark eyes in slum - ber deep _____ .
3. Way, way, way, way, way, way, way, way _____

What is a lullaby?
Why does this music sound like a lullaby?

Melody Instruments

Sing {
D — sol — 5
E — la — 6
G — do — 1
A — re — 2
G — do — 1

MIDDLE C

D E G A

*An Indian syllable coming from the Chippewa word meaning "swaying."

29

The Indian tells of the way he feels in his songs and dances.
He uses many of these in tribal ceremonials.

Play this as an introduction and throughout the song.

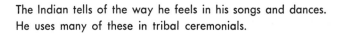

Tom-tom, Drum, or Shakers $\frac{3}{4}$

Magic Feathers

ADAPTED CHIPPEWA SONG

Pi-geon feath-ers, mag-ic feath-ers,
Mi - mi - gwan - ug, de - yo - ha - gi,

Pi-geon feath-ers, mag-ic feath-ers.
Mi - mi - gwan - ug, de - yo - ha - gi.

EAGLE DANCE

Moving in a large circle, flap your arms and take three toe-heel steps to each measure.

toe heel toe heel toe heel

You might like to listen to the CHANT OF THE EAGLE DANCE as performed by the Hopi Indians.

Song of the Peace Pact

ADAPTED CHIPPEWA SONG

Hear, O Chief ___, Hear, O Chief.

Peace from the lead - er from __ Lit - tle Crow.

Walk in peace ___, Walk in peace.

Play both keys at the same time with your right hand, as an introduction, and on the first count of every measure.

MIDDLE C

C   G

Can you find these two piano keys a little lower and play them with your left hand?

Navajo Happy Song

NAVAJO SONG

Hi yo hi yo ip si ni yah,

Hi yo hi yo ip si ni ___ yah, Hi ___ yo

hi yo ip si ni yah, Hi ___ yo

hi yo ip si ni yah ip si ni YAH!

How many times is this used in the song?

Sing
B♭ E♭ E♭ E♭ E♭ E♭
sol do do do do do
5 1 1 1 1 1

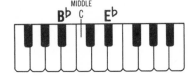

Notice that B♭ and E♭ are played on black keys.

Try making an accompaniment using shakers, gourds, and drums.

32

On the Musical Road
to Storyland

The Nutcracker
and the Mouse King

based upon the story of
E. T. A. Hoffman
with music by

PETER ILYITCH TCHAIKOVSKY

Peter Ilyitch Tchaikovsky was born in Russia, a country where people like to go to the ballet. Russians enjoy watching the dancers in colorful costumes acting out a story to beautiful music. Tchaikovsky wrote the music for some of these stories. One of these was a fairy tale about a little girl's Christmas Eve and a handsome Nutcracker Prince.

PROLOGUE

Overture Miniature

What might this music describe?
Do you think the story it tells will be a happy one?

It is the night before Christmas. New-fallen snow makes the countryside look like a magic land. Inside a large house people are preparing for a Christmas Eve party. Fritz and Marie, with their cousins, wait outside the door of the largest room. Inside this room, mother and father, with the help of uncles and aunts, put the last-minute touches on the tree and presents. The children take turns peeping through the keyhole. As they wait, Marie sees a strange green light shining on the floor. It seems to come from nowhere. She puts her toe into the soft green glow. Since nothing seems to happen she soon forgets all about it.

The doors are opened and mother hands out the gifts. Marie is very happy. One of her gifts is a pair of satin dancing slippers. She quickly puts them on and dances for her family. Soon they all begin to dance.

Just then, in walks the mysterious Dr. Drosselmeyer, Marie's godfather. At first the children are afraid of this strange-looking man and so they hide. He takes off his large black cloak and tosses it into the air. It disappears! Then he calls the children to him. The children come out of their hiding places. He takes out four dolls which dance for the children. Then, like magic, he makes a large wooden nutcracker appear. It is carved in the shape of a soldier and is painted with bright colors. Marie is very pleased when Dr. Drosselmeyer gives her the nutcracker for her very own.

The children play until they become tired and fall asleep. When it is time for the guests to leave they awaken their children and take them home. The nutcracker is placed under the tree and Marie, still sleeping, is carried up to her bed.

THE BATTLE

Marie wakes up thinking about her nutcracker. She tip-toes down the stairs to find it. The tree is in a strange green light! The room is filled with mysterious shadows. The owl on the Grandfather Clock flaps its wings as the clock strikes twelve. The Nutcracker springs to his feet and bows to Marie. The tree begins to grow taller and taller!

Marche

Mice come from every shadow. With them comes the many-headed Mouse King dressed in his gold and purple coat. Just as the mice begin to bother Marie, the Nutcracker calls his army of toy soldiers. The toy cannons and rifles blaze away! The Mouse King and the Nutcracker meet face to face. The Nutcracker is not as strong as the mean Mouse King. Just when all seems lost, Marie pulls off her slipper and strikes the Mouse King to the ground. When the mice see their leader lying there, they run away.

Which theme suggests the toy soldiers? Why?
Which theme suggests the mice? Why?

The Nutcracker stoops to pick up the slipper and is suddenly changed into a handsome Prince. He thanks Marie for saving his life and invites her to his Kingdom of Sweets. With a wave of his arm, the Prince orders a carriage made of half a walnut shell to take Marie to his Kingdom.

THE KINGDOM OF SWEETS

Dance of the Sugar Plum Fairy

The Sugar Plum Fairy sits on her throne in the great palace of the Kingdom of Sweets. She watches the cooks making many fine things to eat. All is made ready to welcome Marie. The beautiful Sugar Plum Fairy comes down from her throne and dances.

What in the music suggests the dancing of the sugar plum?
Why did Tchaikovsky use a bell-like instrument, the celesta, for this dance?

When everything is ready, all the cooks line up to greet Marie and the Nutcracker Prince. The Sugar Plum Fairy introduces Marie to everyone. All of them thank her for saving the life of their Prince. Marie is then asked to join them in their feast. Everyone eats so much that some complain of tummy-aches. Marie tells them of all that has happened since she first saw the pale green light.

The happy little girl is then brought to the throne where she sits beside the Sugar Plum Fairy. They watch dolls from all over the world dance.

Russian Dance

The dancing starts with a group of Cossack dolls dressed in high boots. They do a dance, called the Trepak, which has many squatting steps and high leaps into the air.

What feelings does this music describe?
How would the dancers move to the music?

An important rhythm is:

Play this on a percussion instrument or clap it.

Arabian Dance

The next group of dolls comes from the hot, desert land of Arabia.

What is the tempo of this dance?
Why would a land like Arabia have such a dance?

Chinese Dance

Chinese dolls with folded arms do a stiff dance, taking quick little steps.

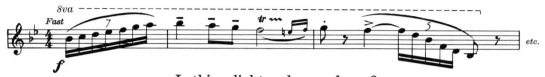

Is this a light or heavy dance?
How is this different from the Russian and Arabian dances?

Dance of the Flutes

Three toy flutes do a little dance as they play a tune.

The brass instruments interrupt this tune. Raise your hand
when you hear them. Raise your hand again when you hear
the flutes take back the tune. How many times do you
hear this happen?

Waltz of the Flowers

The Sugar Plum Fairy calls for the sugar roses that decorate Christmas cakes. She asks them to dance.

The sugar roses enter in small groups until the whole stage is filled with waltzing flowers.

The Prince dances with the Sugar Plum Fairy while the music becomes more and more exciting!

Everyone joins in the final waltz.

As they leave, they make a deep bow to the guest of honor, the proud and happy Marie. The walnut carriage waits to take Marie home. With sweet music still filling their ears, the Prince and the Sugar Plum Fairy bid her good-bye. Marie, filled with happy thoughts, leaves the Kingdom of sweets.

For Marie, this has been the happiest Christmas ever!

Pied Piper of Hamelin

based upon the poem of

Robert Browning

by

DORIS AND WILLIAM FISHER

Long years ago there was a town called Hamelin. Happy children played in the streets. The men and women were hard-working thrifty people. They were very proud of their clean and busy little town. But one day they made a terrible discovery!

Long Years Ago

What does *rit.* tell us to do?

1. Long years a - go in Hame-lin Town, A pret-ty lit - tle cit - y,
2. The peo-ple of old Hame-lin Town, That rat in-fest-ed cit - y,

1. A dread-ful thing had come to pass, It real-ly was a pit - y.
2. Gazed sad - ly 'round them at the town That once had been so pret - ty.

1. For rats had come from all a-round, And ev-'ry-where they could be found.
2. It seemed the rats had come to stay, They sim-ply would not go a - way.

They ate the chees-es in the vats, Made nests in-side men's Sun-day hats,

They e - ven scared a-way the cats! The town was o-ver-run by rats.

First the people were cross, then they were frightened. They rushed to the mayor for help. The mayor called on the town council to do something about getting rid of the rats. No one could think of a thing to do! Then a stranger appeared in town singing a merry tune.

44

The Merry Piper

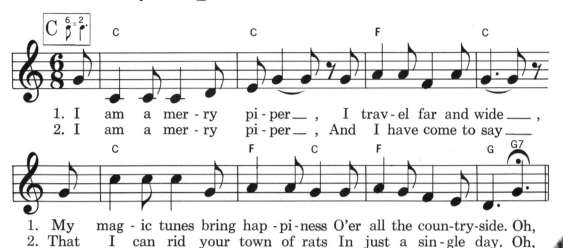

1. I am a mer-ry pi-per___, I trav-el far and wide___,
2. I am a mer-ry pi-per___, And I have come to say___

1. My mag-ic tunes bring hap-pi-ness O'er all the coun-try-side. Oh,
2. That I can rid your town of rats In just a sin-gle day. Oh,

Refrain

Twee-dle dee-dle dee, I play a mer-ry song,

Mak-ing peo-ple hap - py all day long.

3. I am a merry piper, and if you pay my price,
You nevermore will see a sign of any rats or mice. Oh,
Refrain

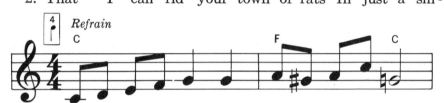

Refrain (Descant for Small Winds or Bells)

C D E F G G F E D D D D C E D F E

Could the Pied Piper really do what he said? The mayor and the council decided they had to take a chance. They had no other choice. The Piper demanded a very high price but the people agreed to pay him what he asked.

The Piper began to play a tune on his pipe. The rats came out of their hiding places to listen. This is what the tune seemed to say:

Rats of Hamelin

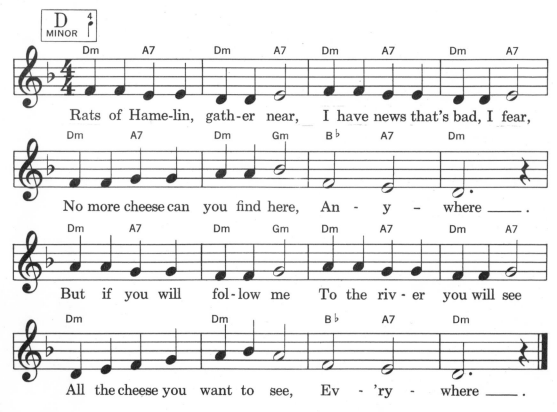

Rats of Hame-lin, gath-er near, I have news that's bad, I fear,

No more cheese can you find here, An - y - where _____ .

But if you will fol-low me To the riv-er you will see

All the cheese you want to see, Ev - 'ry - where _____ .

The rats all followed the Pied Piper to the edge of the river. He stood aside and let them pass. They all jumped into the water and were drowned.

The Piper returned to collect his money. The people would not pay! The price was too high. They knew the rats were gone and could not come back.

Then the Piper began to play a different tune. It was happy music, and all the children came out to listen.

This is what the music said to them:

46

Come with Me

GERMAN FOLK TUNE

Come with me where flow-ers bloom In this love-ly gar - den.

Birds all sing a hap-py tune In this love-ly gar - den.

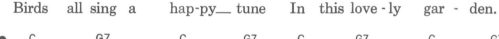

There the sun shines ev-'ry day, Ev -'ry - bod - y feels so gay.

Let's all sing and dance and play In this love-ly gar - den.

Line 1
Make a circle and hold hands. Slide four steps to the left, then four steps to the right.

Line 2
Take seven steps toward the center of the circle and bow. Then take seven steps back.

Line 3
Face your partner. Slap your knees, clap your hands once, and clap your partner's hands twice. Do this again.

Line 4
Repeat Line 1.

47

The Piper walked down the street and out of the town. The children followed as if they could not help themselves. They came to a high mountain. A door in the mountain opened, and the Piper walked through. The dancing, laughing children followed him. The door closed behind them. The selfish people of Hamelin never saw their children again.

In a far-away land some people believe that their grandmothers and grandfathers were these children. These people still hum the tune played by the Pied Piper of Hamelin.

That Merry Man

We love to sing and dance and play

Be - cause a mer-ry pi-per came this way;

He made us hap - py, bright, and gay,

That mer-ry man who came this way.

With My Friends
in Orchestraville

The String Family

A Little Violin

WORDS AND MUSIC BY
HOFFMANN VON FALLERSLEBEN
FREELY TRANSLATED

1. If I on - ly had a vi - o - lin
2. Oh, what love - ly mu - sic I could play!

1. How I would like my lit - tle vi - o - lin.
2. My lit - tle vi - o - lin would sound so sweet.

1. Ev - 'ry day how I would play
2. Friends would come from far and near

1. Mu - sic that would be so gay.
2. When my mu - sic they would hear.

From "Was unsere Kinder Singen." Used by permission of the original publisher,
B. Schott's Soehne, Mainz, and its agent, Associated Music Publishers, Inc., New York.

And sing - ing and danc - ing so hap - py I'd be,

Yes, sing - ing and danc - ing so hap - py I'd be,

Di - del - di - del - dum - dum - dum - dum-dum-dum,

Di - del - di - del - dum - dum - dum - dum - dee.

Listen for the different string instruments on recordings.

Mister 'Cello

MUSIC AND WORDS BY GEORGE MEMBRINO

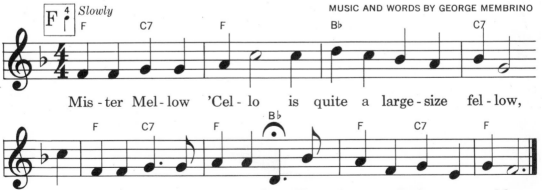

Mis - ter Mel - low 'Cel - lo is quite a large - size fel - low,

You sit to play, his tones are low, He makes sounds that are mel - low.

51

The Clarinet

MUSIC BY DAVID J. ROUSSEAU
WORDS BY PAULINE T. DYER

1. Doo - doo - dle do, da doo - dle day,
2. Some-times the tune is ver - y short,

1. The clar - i - net___ seems to say.
2. Some - times the tune is ver - y long.

1. Its bright hap - py voice brings
2. Each time I hear the voice clari - net

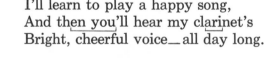

1. Such mer - ry tunes___ our___ way.
2. I want to join___ in its song.

3. Someday I'll have a clarinet,
   I'll learn to play a happy song,
   And then you'll hear my clarinet's
   Bright, cheerful voice___ all day long.

Point to this tune in the song.

Melody Instruments

Sing D   G   D   G   D   G· D   G
     sol do sol do sol do sol do
     5   1   5   1   5   1 5   1

Johnny Schmoker

TRADITIONAL

1-5. John - ny Schmo - ker, John - ny Schmo - ker,

1-5. Can you sing ___ ? Can you play ___ ?

1. I can play up - on my pic - co - lo.
2. I can play up - on my flute ___ .

1. Twee - dle dee - dle oh, so sings my pic - co - lo.
2. Floo - dle floo - dle floo, so sings my flute ___ .

3. . . . clarinet. Doodle doodle det, so sings my clarinet.

4. . . . o-boe. Nono nono no, so sings my o-boe.

5. . . . big bassoon. Noonoo noonoo noon, so sings my big bas-soon.

With each new verse repeat the sounds made by instruments in earlier verses. You could review the string family by adding those instruments to the song. Pretend you are playing the instruments as you sing about them.

As you listen to recordings of the different woodwind instruments, see if you can tell their voices apart.

The Brass Family

The Tuba

W. R. F.
D. R. F.

Oom-pa, oom-pa goes the tu - ba in the big brass band.

Ev - 'ry oom-pa of the tu - ba sounds so big and grand.

Try playing this tune each time you see it in the song.
Sing words to all the other notes.

Melody
Instruments

Sing	C	G	C	G	C	G	F	D
	do	sol	do	sol	do	sol	fa	re
	1	5	1	5	1	5	4	2

What do the dots under
the notes mean?

You might enjoy listening to a recording of TUBBY THE TUBA.

54

My Trumpet

MUSIC AND WORDS BY ELEANOR WEBB LINDQUIST

Oh, root - too - too - too toot   toot is what my trum-pet plays.

Oh, root - too - too - too toot   toot on man - y hap - py days.

I start to play, at break of day, when I get up each morn.

When day is done, I still have fun, just blow-ing on my horn.

Try playing this tune each time you see it in the song. Sing the words to the rest of the song. As you listen to recordings of the different brass instruments, see if you can tell one from another.

Melody Instruments

Sing	G	E	F	G	C	G	E
	sol	mi	fa	sol	do	sol	mi
	5	3	4	5	1	5	3

55

The Big Bass Drum

OLD GAME SONG
TRADITIONAL WORDS

1-3. Oh__, we can play on the
{ 1. big bass drum.
{ 2. tam-bou-rine.
{ 3. tri - an - gle.

1-3. This is the mu - sic to it!

1. Boom, boom, boom goes the big bass drum!
2. Clink, clink, clink goes the tam-bou-rine!
3. Ting, ting, ting goes the tri - an - gle!

1-3. And that is the way we do it.

Other percussion instruments as well as instruments of other families could be added to the song.

With each new verse, repeat the sounds of the instruments in the earlier verses.

56

Play, Tambourine

(Entendez-vous le tambourin)

FOLK SONG FROM FRANCE

Play tam -bour - ine, Say tam - bour - ine,
FRENCH: *En - tend - ez – vous,* *Le tam - bour - in,*

It's time for danc - ing, It's time for danc -ing,
Vite à la dan - se, *Vite à la dan - se,*

Gath - er to - day, Do not de - lay!
En - tend - ez - vous, *Le tam - bour - in,*

O let us join the hap-py throng!
Qui met les vil - la - geois en train!

O let us join the hap-py throng!
Qui met les vil - la - geois en train!

Find the tunes that move by step and those that move by skip.

57

The Orchestra

I Am a Gay Musician

ADAPTED FROM AN OLD SONG

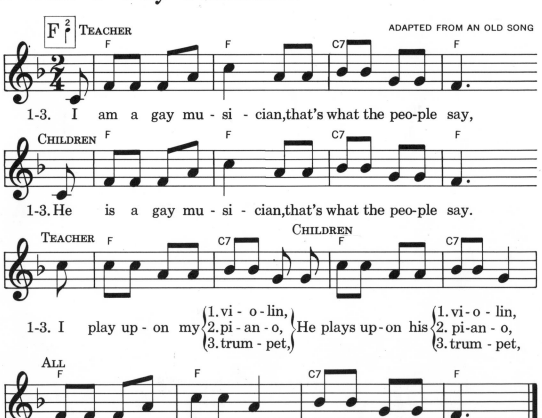

TEACHER

1-3. I am a gay mu - si - cian, that's what the peo-ple say,

CHILDREN

1-3. He is a gay mu - si - cian, that's what the peo-ple say.

TEACHER   CHILDREN

1-3. I play up - on my { 1. vi - o - lin, / 2. pi - an - o, / 3. trum - pet, } He plays up - on his { 1. vi - o - lin, / 2. pi - an - o, / 3. trum - pet,

ALL

1. Fid - dle did - dle did - dle dee,   fid - dle did - dle dee.
2. Plink - a plink - a plink - a plink,   plink - a plink - a plink.
3. Toot toot toot toot toot toot too,   toot toot toot toot too.

58

Do you know the names of some other instruments and how they sound?
Add them to your song.
Which phrases look and sound alike?

How many times can you find this phrase in the song?

Sing	A	B♭	B♭	G	G		F
	mi	fa	fa	re	re		do
	3	4	4	2	2		1

Melody Instruments

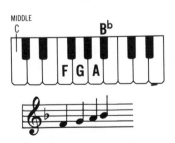

Listen to the recording of RUSTY IN ORCHESTRAVILLE.

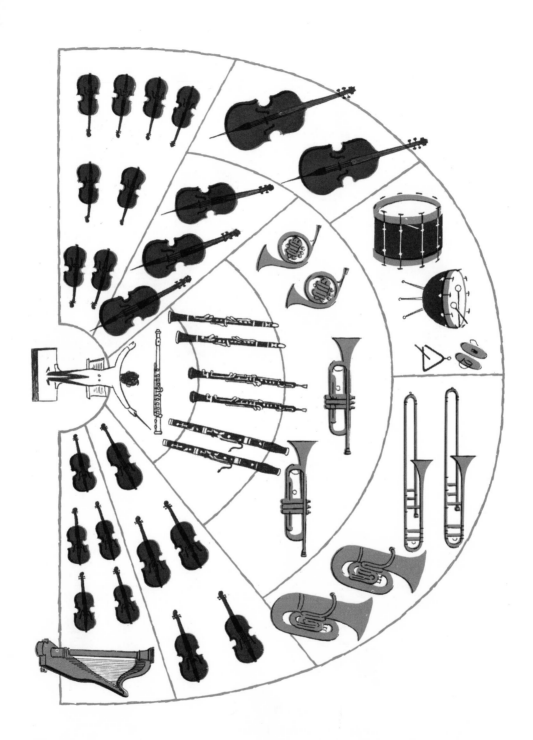

THE SCIENCE OF SOUND

VIBRATING COLUMNS OF AIR

Place different amounts of water in narrow-necked bottles of the same kind and size. Blow across the top of each. Notice the difference in pitch.

What causes this difference in pitch?

Which instruments use this idea in making sound?

Flatten the top of a drinking straw. Cut the corners off the top. Moisten this end of the straw with your mouth. Hold it between closed lips and blow.

What happens when you shorten the straw a little at a time?

Which instruments use this idea to make their sound?

VIBRATING STRINGS

Stretch a rubber band tightly between your hands. Have someone pluck the rubber band. Do you notice that it moves something like this?

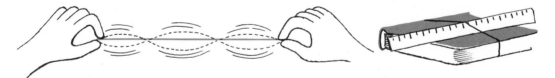

Place a rubber band around a book. Put a ruler on its edge on one side of the book under the rubber band. Have someone pluck the rubber band.

What happens to the sound? Why?

Place one finger on the rubber band. Pluck the rubber band. Now move your finger closer to the ruler and pluck the rubber band again.

What do you notice?

Which instruments use this idea to make their sound?

Peter and the Wolf

by

SERGE PROKOFIEV

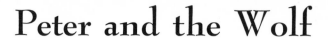

Peter and the Wolf is a Russian fairy tale told by the orchestra with the help of a story teller. As you listen to this musical story you will find that each character is played by an instrument in the orchestra.

PETER

Why does the composer use the string quartet to play the part of Peter?

THE BIRD

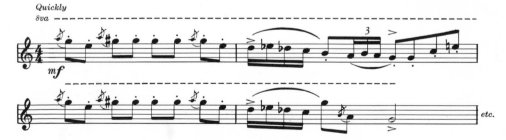

Why does he have the flute play the part of the bird?

62

THE DUCK

Why does the composer have the oboe play the part of the duck?

THE CAT

Why does he have the clarinet play the part of the cat?

THE GRANDFATHER

Why does he have the bassoon play the part of the grandfather?

THE WOLF

Why does the composer use three horns to play the part of the wolf?

THE SHOOTING OF THE HUNTERS

Why does he have the kettle drums and bass drum play the music for the shooting of the hunters?

When All Nature Sings

Let Us Go Walking

MUSIC AND WORDS BY
MARIE E. GAUDETTE

With a light, lilting tempo

1. Let us go walk-ing to-geth - er,
2. Let us be sing-ing to-geth - er,

1. Let us go walk-ing to-geth - er,
2. Let us be sing-ing to-geth - er,

1. Through wood and mead-ow o'er hill and dale,
2. With round and bal-lad and roun-de-lay,

1. Let us go walk-ing to-geth - er.
2. Let us be sing-ing to-geth - er.

Try strolling, taking two steps to a measure.

Sticks
Blocks

Jingle Bells
Triangle

The Forest at Dawn

SWEDISH FOLK TUNE
WORDS BY DORIS R. FISHER

The for-est at the dawn-ing is still___ fast a - sleep
He sings to greet the morn-ing, his song___ fills the air,

When soft on the air___ comes a bird's first peep.
He calls to the sleep - y - heads___ ev - 'ry - where.

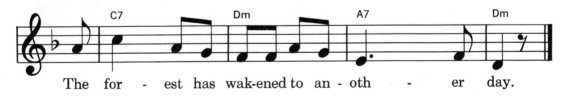

"Wake up, the day is break - ing, Look up and see the sun
Sing out, the world is wak - ing, A new day has be - gun!"

Now all the woods are stir - ring, All na - ture seems to say

The for - est has wak-ened to an - oth - er day.

Melody Instruments

Sing { A D E F G A
       mi la ti do re mi
       3 6 7 1 2 3

How many times can you find this tune in the song?

God Has Created a New Day

MUSIC AND WORDS BY
MARIE E. GAUDETTE

God has cre - a - ted a new day, Sil - ver and green and gold;

Live that the sun - set may find us Wor -thy His gift to hold.

A few might like to play this melody while the class sings.

Melody Instruments

C B A G A E E F G E

These are first and second endings.   1.   2.

Do not play the first ending the second time through the song.

Under the Spreading Chestnut Tree

OLD ENGLISH SONG
WORDS ADAPTED

1-4. Un - der   the spread - ing   chest - nut   tree;

1. In   the   shade   just   you   and   me,
2. We   will   nev - er   dis - a - gree,
3. Where   the   air   is   pure   and   free,
4. What   a   love - ly   place   to   be,

1-4. Oh   how   hap - py   we   will   be,

1-4. Un - der   the spread - ing   chest - nut   tree.

Try the following actions as you sing.

"Under"   — (bend down)
"spreading" — (spread arms wide apart)
"chest"   — (slap chest)
"nut"   — (tap head)
"tree"   — (flutter outstretched arms)

In some games there is a home base. In music this home base is called the home tone or key tone. A song is built around this key tone. Usually it is the final note of the song. What is the pitch name of the last note in this song?

Using both hands, show how the melody of this tune moves.

Melody Instruments

Sing	C	B	A	G
	do	ti	la	sol
	8	7	6	5

69

Play this as others sing the song.

7 ti 8 do 8 do 7 ti
6 la 6 la
5 sol 5 sol
3 mi 4 fa 4 fa 3 mi
2 re 2 re
1 do 1 do

C D E F G A B C C B A G F E D C
(half step) (half step) (half step) (half step)

Spring Flowers

SCALE SONG
WORDS BY ANNE KAELIN

C

C   G7   C   F

I love all the flow-ers With col-ors so gay

C   F   G7   C

That bloom in the spring-time And bright-en the day.

C   E7   F   C

In gar-dens and mead-ows At this time of year

F   C   G7   C

They bring us a mes-sage Of glad-ness and cheer.

Can You Plant the Seeds?

(Savez-vous planter les choux?)

ADAPTED FOLK SONG FROM FRANCE

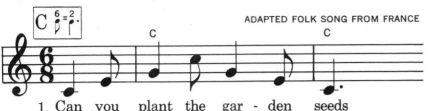

1. Can you plant the gar - den seeds
FRENCH: *Sa - vez - vous plant - er les choux,**

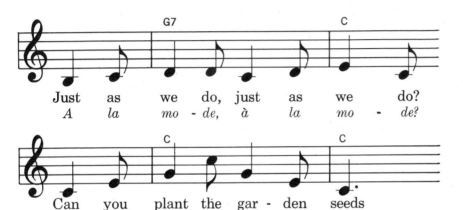

Just as we do, just as we do?
A la mo - de, à la mo - de?

Can you plant the gar - den seeds
Sa - vez - vous plant - er les choux,

Just the same as we can do?
A la mo - de de chez nous?

2. People plant them with their feet,
   (On les plant avec le pied,)
   Just as we do, just as we do, . . .
   (A la mode, a la mode, . . .)

Play this each time you see it in the song.

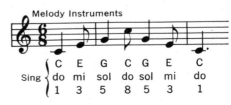

Melody Instruments

Sing
C E G C G E C
do mi sol do sol mi do
1 3 5 8 5 3 1

*choux really means "cabbages."

The Narcissus
(Sui Sin Fa)

CHINESE FOLK TUNE
WORDS ADAPTED

Play throughout:

Finger Cymbals

Fair nar - cis - sus ____ , sui sin ____ fa,

Love - ly ____ blos - som ____ , sui sin ____ fa,

Send - ing fra - grance ____ through the air,

No oth - er flow - er ____ can com - pare.

The Narcissus

(Percussion Score)

X = Gong

Rabbit in the Wood

OLD SONG
SOURCE UNKNOWN

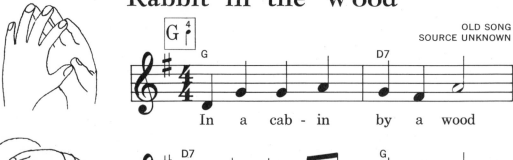

In a cab - in by a wood

Lit - tle man by the win - dow stood,

Saw a rab - bit hop - ping by,

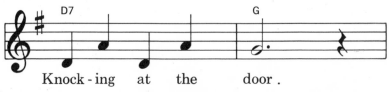

Knock - ing at the door.

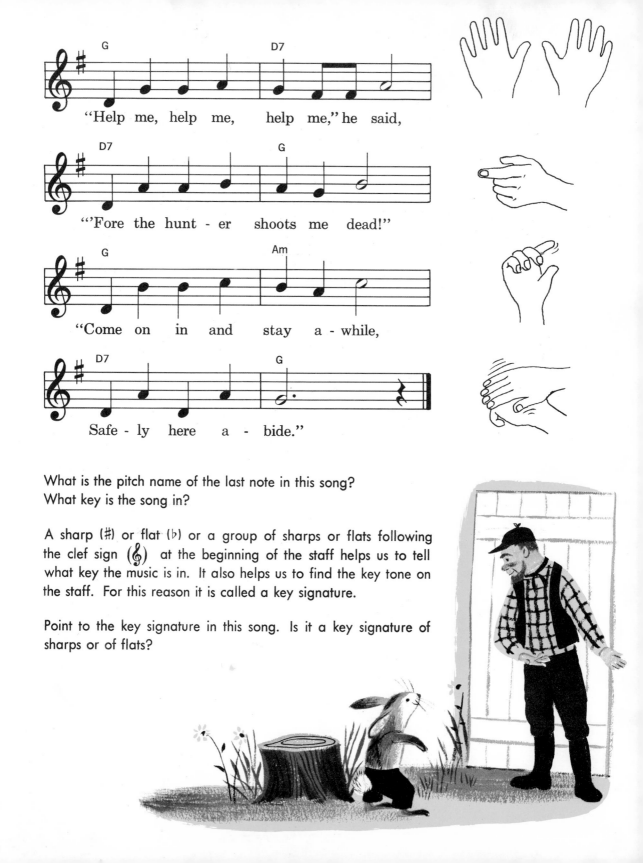

"Help me, help me, help me," he said,

"'Fore the hunt - er shoots me dead!"

"Come on in and stay a - while,

Safe - ly here a - bide."

What is the pitch name of the last note in this song?
What key is the song in?

A sharp (♯) or flat (♭) or a group of sharps or flats following
the clef sign (𝄞) at the beginning of the staff helps us to tell
what key the music is in. It also helps us to find the key tone on
the staff. For this reason it is called a key signature.

Point to the key signature in this song. Is it a key signature of
sharps or of flats?

The Contest

MUSIC BY CARL F. ZELTER
WORDS BY VON FALLERSLEBEN
FREELY TRANSLATED

1. The cuck-oo and the don-key
2. "I'll show you," said the cuck-oo,

1. A - greed to have a test,
2. But screams were all he made,

1. One _ love-ly day in May ____,
2. "Oh ___, I can sing much bet - ter,

1. One _ love-ly day in May ____,
2. Oh ___, I can sing much bet - ter,"

1. To   see   who   sang   the   best _____ ,
2. The   don - key   loud - ly   brayed _____ ,

1. To   see   who   sang   the   best .
2. The   don - key   loud - ly   brayed .

3. They sounded so delightful
   They said they'd fight no more.
   They sang along togeth-er,
   They sang along togeth-er,
   Cuckoo, cuckoo, heehaw,
   Cuckoo, cuckoo, heehaw.

Find this tune in the song:

Melody Instruments						
Sing	B♭	A	A	G	G	F
	fa	mi	mi	re	re	do
	4	3	3	2	2	1

The Cuckoo

FOLK SONG FROM AUSTRIA
ENGLISH VERSION BY GLADYS PITCHER

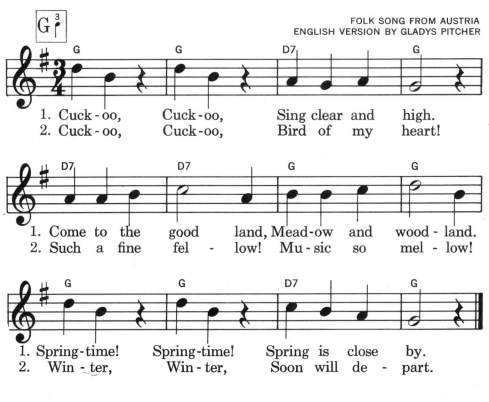

1. Cuck-oo, Cuck-oo, Sing clear and high.
2. Cuck-oo, Cuck-oo, Bird of my heart!

1. Come to the good land, Mead-ow and wood-land.
2. Such a fine fel - low! Mu - sic so mel - low!

1. Spring-time! Spring-time! Spring is close by.
2. Win - ter, Win - ter, Soon will de - part.

Can you find the key signature in this song?
Is it a key signature of sharps or flats?

Find the key signature in other songs you have sung.
Are they key signatures of sharps or flats?

Try to play these notes each time you see them in the song.
Sing words to all the other notes.

Melody Instruments

Sing { D B
       sol mi
       5   3

MIDDLE C

B D

The Donkey

OLD ROUND

I
Sweet-ly sings the don-key at the break of day;

II
If you do not feed him, this is what he'll say,

III
(Place thumbs to ears and wave fingers)
"Hee - haw! Hee - haw! Hee - haw! Hee-haw! Hee-haw!"

When there is a flat (♭) or a group of flats in the key signature,
the last flat is called "fa," or 4 of the scale.
Beginning with that line or space as "fa," or 4, count down to
"do," or 1. This is the key tone.

How many flats are there in the key signature of this song?
On which line or space is the last flat?
Where on the staff is the key tone?
In what key is this song written?

Old MacDonald

TRADITIONAL

1-3. Old Mac-Don-ald had a farm, Ee - i - ee - i - o,

1-3. And on that farm he had some
{ 1. chicks,
2. ducks,
3. pigs, }
Ee - i - ee - i - o.

1. With a chick-chick here, and a chick - chick there,
2. With a quack-quack here, and a quack - quack there,
3. With an oink - oink here, and an oink - oink there,

1. Here a chick, there a chick, ev - 'ry-where a chick - chick,
2. Here a quack, there a quack, ev - 'ry-where a quack - quack,
3. Here an oink, there an oink, ev - 'ry-where an oink - oink,

1-3. Old Mac-Don-ald had a farm, Ee - i - ee - i - o.

Can you think of other animals to sing about?
With each new verse repeat the sounds made by the animals in earlier verses.

Old MacDonald

(Percussion Score)

When there is a sharp (♯) or a group of sharps in the key signature, the last sharp is called "ti," or 7 of the scale. The next tone above is "do," or 8 (the key tone).

Find the last sharp in the key signature. What tone of the scale is it? What is the pitch name of the next tone up? What key is the song in?

81

Down the River

AMERICAN PLAY PARTY SONG

1-3. The riv-er is up, and the chan-nel is deep,

1-3. The wind is stead-y and strong _____ ,

1. Oh, won't we have a jol-ly good time,
2. Oh, Di - nah, put the hoe - cake on,
3. The waves do splash from shore ___ to shore,

1-3. As we go sail-ing a - long _____ .

Refrain

Down the riv - er, oh, down the riv - er,

Oh, down the riv - er we go - o - o;

Down the riv - er, oh, down the riv - er,

Oh, down the O - hi - o ____ !

The River

OLD SONG ADAPTED

1. Slow-ly flow-ing, great wide riv-er, Al-ways flow-ing, mov-ing on,
2. Wind-ing, turn-ing, to the o - cean, Mov-ing out so grace-ful - ly;

1. Down the hill - side, through the val - ley, Mov-ing stead-i - ly a - long.
2. Ev - er grow-ing large and larg-er, Mov-ing on out to the sea.

Point to the last sharp in the key signature.
What tone of the scale is it?
What is the pitch name of the next tone up?
What key is the song in?

The Carnival of the Animals

by

CAMILLE SAINT-SAËNS

Saint-Saëns was born over one hundred years ago in Paris, France. When he was a little boy he was interested in all kinds of sounds. He loved to imitate them—the clanging of bells, the whistling of the teakettle, and the sounds of birds and animals. Have you ever tried making the sounds of birds and animals? Was it fun? Saint-Saëns thought it was.

When he grew older he learned about the instruments of the orchestra—how they are played and how they sound. He wrote music which used these instruments to imitate sounds of animals and to suggest how they look and act. Once, for carnival time in Paris, he put these sounds together for a concert. He named this music *The Carnival of the Animals*.

Every carnival needs a master of ceremonies. Saint-Saëns chose the piano as master of ceremonies because he liked the piano and played it very well. The piano is in complete charge of *The Carnival of the Animals*.

INTRODUCTION

Have you ever been to a zoo? Perhaps, near the entrance, you saw a sign that said "To the Animals." You didn't really need this sign because your ears told you that the animals were near.

Let's listen now to the introduction. Does it sound as if all the animals are talking at once? What happens as you get closer to the cages? How does Saint-Saëns show this? Listen now as everything grows quiet and we hear music that calls our attention to the ROYAL MARCH OF THE LIONS.

ROYAL MARCH OF THE LIONS

What does Saint-Saëns do in the music to attract our attention? Which instrument plays this?

Here, in his royal fur collar, is the lion, mighty King of Beasts!

Which instruments are used to play this part?
How does the music suggest the lion?

Can you hear any short growls played by the strings?
Are these growls loud or soft?
How can you tell this by looking at the music?

Before the lion disappears we hear one last mighty roar from His Royal Highness.

This roar seems to glide up and down. How is this pictured on the staff?
What tells the musicians to make the music grow louder, then softer?
Which instruments are used to make this last roar?

HENS AND COCKS

Can you hear the hens and cocks cackling?

Which instrument do you hear?

85

Listen to the cocks stepping along so proudly.

Which family of instruments do you hear?

Let's hear the cocks' proud call, "Cock-a-doodle-do!"

Which instrument do you think was used to play this tune?
Wasn't that good!

The hens keep saying, "Cut-cut-cut-cut-
cut-cut-ca-daw-cut."

Which instruments are used to play this?

WILD DONKEYS

These wild donkeys move with great speed, kicking and bucking,
but never seem to get anywhere. Can you hear them?

86

TURTLES

Hear how slowly the strings play this tune.
Try singing this melody on "loo" at a fast speed.
Now sing it as turtles might move to it.
See what a difference speed makes?
This difference of speed is called *tempo*.

Try walking and running to this rhythm in slow turtle tempo.
Now try it in a faster tempo.

THE ELEPHANT

Every carnival needs a funny-man. Can you imagine an elephant
dressed in short frilly skirts trying to do a toe dance? Well, here he is!

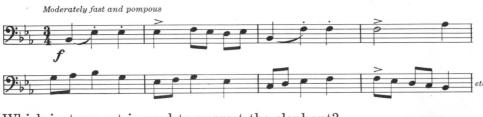

Which instrument is used to suggest the elephant?
Try moving to this music as an elephant might.

KANGAROOS

We all know how kangaroos move. They hop like this:

They jump like this:

pp

Did you hear the difference? Listen to the music again. Raise your right hand when you hear the kangaroo hop and your left hand when you hear him jump. Now try hopping and jumping to this music.

AQUARIUM

Have you ever seen beautiful fish swimming back and forth in an aquarium? They seem to move with hardly a sound. The water moves too. Can you imagine what this very soft sound would be like if our ears could hear it?

Perhaps it would be like this:

Moderately (not too fast)

pp

Which instruments did you hear? There are three. Which instrument was used to suggest the rippling water?

LONG-EARED PERSONS

Everyone knows this animal. He is the kicking mule with his silly laugh, "Hee-haw!"

8va

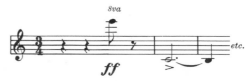

ff

Guess which instrument made this silly sound! It is hard to believe that the beautiful violin could make such a sound, but it did.

THE CUCKOO IN THE FOREST

Pretend that you are in the deep woods. When all seems to be still, we can hear a small voice. It is the cuckoo. Poor fellow, all he can say is his own name over and over again, "Cuckoo, cuckoo."

Which instrument plays this call?
Are these notes short or long? How is this marked?

AVIARY

An aviary in a zoo is such a large bird cage that it seems to be a part of the out-of-doors. This is no quiet place — not for a moment! One little bird can be heard above all the others:

Which instrument makes this sound? Why?

FOSSILS

Fossils are signs of things that lived a long time ago. Leaf prints in stones are fossils. Imprints of animal bones are fossils too. Some of them have been buried in the earth for millions of years. Perhaps Saint-Saëns thought some tunes were played so often that they seemed old, like fossils. He used some of these tunes to suggest fossils. One tune was his own DANSE MACABRE which is played so often at Halloween:

Another tune was this one:

Do you know the name of this?

THE SWAN

How beautiful and how graceful is the swan! Again we hear the piano making sounds like rippling water. At the same time a solo instrument plays the part of the smoothly gliding swan.

Can you tell to what family this instrument belongs?
Which instrument is it?
How is it different from some of the other members of this family?

FINALE

As the carnival comes to an end, we hear the same sounds of the zoo which we heard at the beginning. If you listen carefully, you will recognize some of the animals who appear once again to bid us farewell.

Magic
of Faraway Places

This Wide World
(Turn the Glasses Over)

ENGLISH PLAY-PARTY GAME
AMERICAN VERSION

I've been to Har - lem,   I've   been to Do - ver,
(Partners walk in circle.)

I've trav-eled this   wide   world   all   o - ver,

O - ver,   o - ver,   three   times   o - ver,

Drink   all the lem - on - ade and   turn the glass-es   o - ver
(Both turn under arms.)

92

Refrain

Sail - ing east, sail - ing west,

(Inner circle change direction.)

Sail - ing o - ver the o - cean,

Bet - ter watch out when the boat be - gins to rock,

Or you'll lose your girl in the o - cean.

(Boys take nearest girl for new partner.)

Those who are left without a partner will go to the center.

You can use the names of other cities in the first line.

How many times can you find these notes (G, E, D) in the song?

Melody
Instruments

Sing
G	G	G	E	D
do	do	do	la	sol
1	1	1	6	5

The Happy Wanderer

MUSIC BY FRIEDRICH W. MÖLLER
WORDS BY ANTONIA RIDGE

1. I love to go a-wan-der-ing,
2. I love to wan-der by the stream

1. A-long the moun-tain track,
2. That danc-es in the sun,

1. And as I go, I love to sing,
2. So joy-ous-ly it calls to me,

1. My knap-sack on my back.
2. "Come! join my hap-py song."

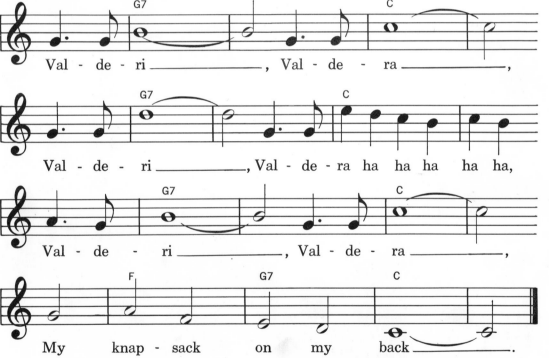

Refrain

Val - de - ri _____, Val - de - ra _____,

Val - de - ri _____, Val - de - ra ha ha ha ha ha,

Val - de - ri _____, Val - de - ra _____,

My knap - sack on my back _____.

3. I wave my hat to all I meet,
   And they wave back to me,
   And blackbirds call so loud and sweet
   From every greenwood tree.
   Refrain

4. High overhead, the skylark wing,
   They never rest at home
   But just like me, they love to sing,
   As o'er the world we roam.
   Refrain

The Silver Rocket Ship

MUSIC BY WILLIAM R. FISHER
WORDS BY DORIS R. FISHER

1. In the sil - ver rock - et ship   Ev-'ry-thing is read - y,
2. As - tro-nauts who fly so high, New worlds to dis - cov - er,

1. Space - men   ea - ger for   the trip   Wait-ing, strong and stead - y.
2. What strange won-ders of   the sky   Will this trip un - cov - er?

1. Ten, nine, eight, seven, six, five, four,   Just a few brief mo-ments more,
2. Soon their rock- et ship will   race   Head-long in - to out - er space,

1. Three, two, one, the time has come,   Ze-ro, BLAST OFF!
2. Three, two, one, the time has come,   Ze-ro, BLAST OFF!

Our Borders North and South

Mother Mouse Hawk's Lullaby

ESKIMO SONG
AS SUNG TO ROXIE K. BERGH
TRANSLATED BY EMILY I. BROWN

The riv-er's so wide, The riv-er's so cold,

I must fly as fast as we can _____,

Try to be a brave bird ___, Hold, on ver-y tight-ly,

Hold on so tight-ly, as we land.

Can you find this tune in the song?

Melody Instruments

Sing:
	D	D	A	G	A
	la	la	mi	re	mi
	6	6	3	2	3

The Eskimo children in Alaska learn about Mother Mouse Hawk's moving her children across the flooding and rising river to a safe and dry place. She sings this song to them during the dangerous trip. The children are quieted down and forget the perils of their journey.

97

The Igloo

FOLK TUNE FROM CANADA
WORDS BY ELINOR WARNER

The first cou-ple out to the cou-ple on the right,

And take a look at the north-ern lights,

In - to the ig - loo by the door

And clap your hands then clap all four!

Out of the ig - loo and in - to the ring,

And give your hon - ey a great big swing!

98

Alouette

FRENCH CANADIAN FOLK SONG

Refrain

A - lou - et - te,   gen - tille A - lou - et - te,

Fine

A - lou - et - te,   Je te plu - me - rai.

Verse

LEADER   CLASS

1. Je te plu - me - rai la tête, Je te plu - me - rai la tête,
2. Je te plu - me - rai le bec,   Je te plu - me - rai le bec,

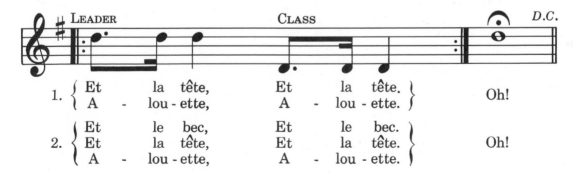

LEADER   CLASS   D.C.

1. { Et   la tête,   Et   la tête. }   Oh!
   { A - lou - ette,   A - lou - ette. }

2. { Et   le bec,   Et   le bec. }
   { Et   la tête,   Et   la tête. }   Oh!
   { A - lou - ette,   A - lou - ette. }

3. Le nez   4. Le dos   5. Les pattes   6. Le cou
   (*the nose*)   (*the back*)   (*the claws*)   (*the neck*)

   (La tête—*the head*)   (Le bec—*the beak*)

99

Chiapanecas*

MEXICAN CLAP DANCE
VERSES BY ANNE KAELIN

Here is a ver-y good way, good way
Refrain: Oh, Chia - pa - ne - cas, ay, ay! (clap, clap)

You can be hap-py and gay, and gay;
Oh, Chia - pa - ne - cas, ay, ay! (clap, clap)

Ev - 'ry - one fol - low a - long, a - long,
Oh, Chia - pa - ne - cas, ay, ay! (clap, clap)

Lift up your voi-ces in song_____ .
Oh, Chia-pa - ne-cas, ay, ay! O - le!

(SPEAK)

Sticks
Wood Blocks

Jingle Bells
Triangles

Sticks
Wood Blocks

Sticks
Jingle Bells
Wood Blocks
Triangles

*Pronounced: Cha-pah-<u>neh</u>-kas

✕ = Cymbals

100

Going to the Fair

FOLK DANCE FROM GERMANY
WORDS ADAPTED

1. When the fa-ther and the moth-er take their fam-'ly to the fair,
Lit-tle mon-ey in their pock-ets and it's lit-tle that they care.

(Walk with partners in a double ring, girls on the inside.)

Ach, ja! Ach, ja!
(Bow to partner.) *(Bow to neighbor.)*

Refrain

Tra la la, Tra la la, Tra la la la la la la,
(Turn partner, right hands or elbows joined.)

Tra la la, Tra la la, Tra la la la la la la!
(Turn partner, left hands or elbows joined.)

Ach, ja! Ach, ja!
(Bow to partner.) *(Boys move forward to new partner.)*

2. Then they meet their friends and neighbors with their children on the way,
Ach, ja! Ach, ja!
And they greet them with a smile and stop to chat about the day,
Ach, ja! Ach, ja!
Refrain

101

My Hat
(Mein Hut)

GERMAN FOLK SONG

My hat   it   has   three   cor-ners_____,
GERMAN: *Mein Hut   er   hat   drei   Eck - en_____,*

Three   cor -   ners   has   my   hat_____;
Drei   Eck -   en   hat   mein   Hut_____;

And   had   it   not   three   cor-ners_____,
Und   hätt   er   nicht   drei   Eck - en_____,

It   would   not   be   my   hat_____.
Dann   ist   er   nicht   mein   Hut_____.

Where is this tune in the song?

Melody Instruments

Sing	E mi 3	F fa 4	G sol 5	A la 6	B ti 7	C do 8 ___

Can you do actions to
the song as you sing?

"My"   — (point to yourself)
"hat"   — (touch your head)
"three"   — (hold up three fingers)
"corners" — (make a corner with
both hands, fingers touching)

102

Lullaby
(Wiegenlied)

MUSIC BY JOHANNES BRAHMS
· TRADITIONAL WORDS

Tenderly

Lull - a - by and good night, With___ ros - es be-dight___,
GERMAN: *Gu - ten A - bend, gut' Nacht, Mit___ Ros - en be - dacht___,*

With___ lil - ies o'er___ spread, Is___ ba - by's wee bed.
Mit___ Näg - lein be - steckt, Schlupf___ un - ter die Deck.

Lay thee down now and rest, May thy slum-bers be blest;
Mor - gen früh, wenn Gott will, Wirst du wie - der ge - weckt;

Lay thee down now and rest, May thy slum-bers be blest.
Mor - gen früh, wenn Gott will, Wirst du wie - der ge - weckt.

Melody Instruments

Sing { E E G E E G
mi mi sol mi mi sol
3 3 5 3 3 5

Can you find this tune in the song?

sol   sol

mi   mi   mi   mi

103

One - Two - Three

TYROLESE FOLK TUNE, ADAPTED
WORDS BY ALBERT W. WASSELL

One, two, three, glide a - long, Dance_to the mu - sic.

One, two, three, sing a song, Clap_hands and sway.

When-e'er we dance this way, Our hearts are made more gay;

One, two, three, glide a - long, Sing - ing this song.

Melody Instruments

Sing { E   E   E   E   G   G
       mi mi mi   mi sol sol
       3   3   3   3   5   5

Try playing these notes each time
you see them in the song. Sing words
to all the other notes.

Making up a dance to this tune might
be fun.

104

Doing Nothing but Sing

ALSATIAN FOLK TUNE
OLD ENGLISH RHYME

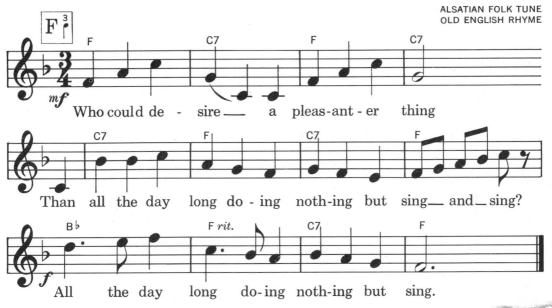

Who could de - sire — a pleas-ant-er thing

Than all the day long do-ing noth-ing but sing — and — sing?

All the day long do-ing noth-ing but sing.

As you tap to the meter, sing "tah" to the following measures, repeating each a number of times:

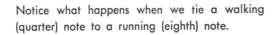

Notice what happens when we tie a walking (quarter) note to a running (eighth) note.

This is another way of writing the same rhythm. Can you find two measures in the song that have this for their rhythm?

Read the words of these measures in rhythm.

105

Frère Jacques
(Are You Sleeping?)

ROUND FROM FRANCE

FRENCH: Frè - re   Jac - ques!   Frè - re   Jac - ques!
Are   you   sleep - ing,   Are   you   sleep - ing,

Dor - mez   vous?   Dor - mez   vous?
Broth - er   John,   Broth - er   John?

Son - nez   les   ma - ti - nes,   Son - nez   les   ma - ti - nes,
Morn - ing   bells   are   ring - ing,   Morn - ing   bells   are   ring - ing,

Din,   din,   don!   Din,   din,   don!

Some might like to play this song on the autoharp.
It is very easy. It has only one chord to strum.

106

Sur le pont d'Avignon

(On the Bridge of Avignon)

CHILDREN'S SONG FROM FRANCE

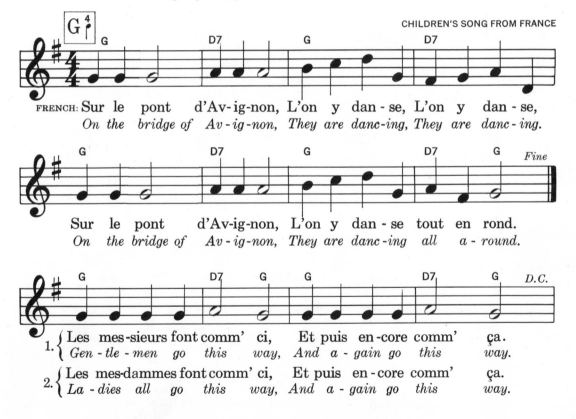

FRENCH: Sur le pont d'Av-ig-non, L'on y dan-se, L'on y dan-se,
On the bridge of Av-ig-non, They are danc-ing, They are danc-ing.

Sur le pont d'Av-ig-non, L'on y dan-se tout en rond.
On the bridge of Av-ig-non, They are danc-ing all a-round.

1. Les mes-sieurs font comm' ci, Et puis en-core comm' ça.
   Gen-tle-men go this way, And a-gain go this way.
2. Les mes-dammes font comm' ci, Et puis en-core comm' ça.
   La-dies all go this way, And a-gain go this way.

Some of you might like to play the autoharp while others sing this song.
It uses two chords G and D7. Strum twice to a measure.

107

My Farm
(*Mi chacra*)

FOLK SONG FROM ARGENTINA
TRANSLATED BY OLCUTT AND PHYLLIS SANDERS

Come, come and see my farm for it is love - ly.

SPANISH: *Ven - gan a ver mi cha - cra que es her - mo - sa.*

Come, come and see my farm for it is love - ly.

Ven - gan a ver mi cha - cra que es her - mo - sa.

El po - lli - to goes like this: peep peep,

El po - lli - to hace a - sí: pipi - ri,

(SPEAK)

El po - lli - to goes like this: peep peep.

El po - lli - to hace a - sí: pipi - ri.

(SPEAK)

Refrain

O vas, cam-a - rad - a, vas cam-a - rad - a, vas, O vas, O vas,

O vas, cam-a - rad - a, vas cam-a - rad - a, vas, O vas, O vas.

Carrousel

SWEDISH PLAY SONG

1. How we love to ride the car - rou - sel,
2. While we're rid - ing on the car - rou - sel,

(Girls circle left 2 steps to a measure-Boys with hands on girls' shoulders.)

1. 'Round and 'round ad-vanc - ing, on our po - nies pranc - ing.
2. Up and down we're bounc-ing, in the sad - dle jounc - ing.

1. Cam - els, ze - bras, el - e -phants as well
2. An - y time you hear the start - ing bell

1. Greet us on the car - rou - sel.
2. Join us on the car - rou - sel.
(Stamp) (Stamp) (Stamp)

Faster

1&2. Ha, ha, ha! Hap- py are we.

(Slide left four times each measure. On repeat slide right.)

1&2. An - der - son and Hen-der - son and Lund-strom and me.

(Partners change places, then repeat the dance.)

My Gondola

ITALIAN FOLK TUNE
WORDS BY DORIS R. FISHER

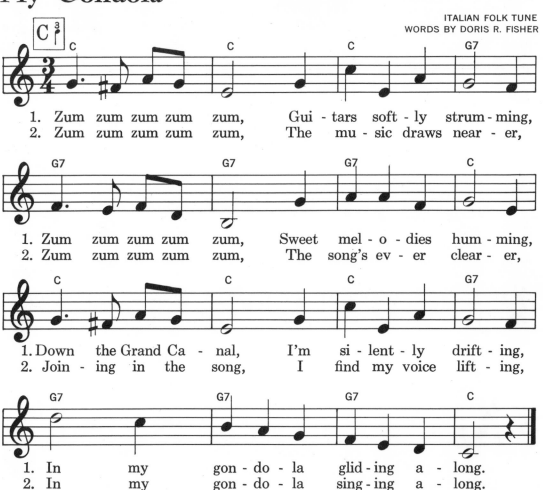

1. Zum zum zum zum zum, Gui - tars soft - ly strum - ming,
2. Zum zum zum zum zum, The mu - sic draws near - er,

1. Zum zum zum zum zum, Sweet mel - o - dies hum - ming,
2. Zum zum zum zum zum, The song's ev - er clear - er,

1. Down the Grand Ca - nal, I'm si - lent - ly drift - ing,
2. Join - ing in the song, I find my voice lift - ing,

1. In my gon - do - la glid - ing a - long.
2. In my gon - do - la sing - ing a - long.

As the class sings the song some of you could play the rhythm
on resonator bells or hand bells:

Group I play the C chord (C E G)

Group II play the G7 chord (G B D F)

Pretend you are strumming a guitar.

110

On the Islands

Tinga Layo

Play this throughout the song.

Maracas
Claves
Drum

CALYPSO SONG FROM THE WEST INDIES

1&2. Tin - ga Lay - o! Come, lit - tle don - key, come;

1&2. Tin - ga Lay - o! Come, lit - tle don - key, come.

1. My don - key walk, my don - key talk, my
2. My don - key eat, my don - key sleep, my

1. don - key eat with a knife and fork.
2. don - key kick with his two hind feet.

1&2. Tin - ga Lay - o! Come, lit - tle don - key, come;

1&2. Tin - ga Lay - o! Come, lit - tle don - key, come.

My Boat

FOLK SONG FROM HAWAII
COLLECTED AND ADAPTED BY
ERMINE AND ELSA CROSS

My boat is sail - ing, sail - ing___, sail - ing,

My boat is sail - ing o - ver the wa - ter.

My boat is sail - ing, sail - ing___, sail - ing,

My boat is sail - ing o - ver the sea___.

112

Refrain

| D7 | | G |

Will you go with me? Will you go with me?

| | D7 | | G |

Will you go with me o - ver the wa - ter?

| | D7 | | G |

Yes, I'll go with you, Yes, I'll go with you,

| | D7 | | G |

Yes, I'll go with you o - ver the sea _____ .

Some of you might like to play a rhythmic descant with Hawaiian puili (poo-*ee*-lee) sticks while sitting cross-legged or kneeling on the floor.

TAP: palm, floor, shoulder, partner's stick.

Can you tell the story of this song with your hands? Look at the pictures on page 112 for a few suggestions.

The hula is a dance that tells a story. The dancer tells the meaning of the words with the hands or arms. Native Hawaiians usually sway their hips as their arms and hands keep moving from one motion to another.

113

Dancing the Merengue

PUERTO RICAN FOLK SONG
MUSIC AND WORDS ADAPTED

1. Ma - ra - cas   are play - ing, Danc-ers   are sway - ing
2. song is   in - vit - ing, Hear the   ex - cit - ing

1. In   a   Mer - en - gue   gay;
2. Trop - i - cal mu - sic   play;

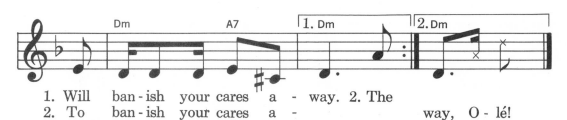

1. Just   give   it   a chance, this   trop - i - cal   dance
2. So   join in   the dance, and   give   it   a   chance

1. Will   ban - ish your cares   a - way. 2. The
2. To   ban - ish   your cares   a -   way, O - lé!

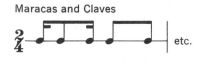

Maracas and Claves

etc.

BASIC DANCE STEP
Step left, step together,
Bend knees slightly.
Dance in a large single circle.

PART II

Let's Make More Music

WITH SMALL WINDS AND AUTOHARP

A BEGINNING RHYTHM

Beat with the palm of your hand as you read aloud the words below.

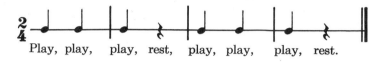

Play, play, play, rest, play, play, play, rest.

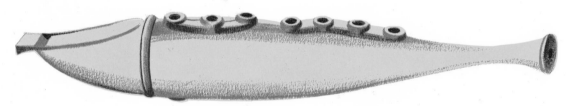

OUR FIRST NOTE

Put your left thumb on the thumb hole (T) and your first finger on the first hole (1). Blow gently.

Play by blowing once for each note.
At the rest sign say "rest."

This note is B.

B

B B   B (rest) B B   B (rest)

Some of you might like to strum the autoharp while others play on small winds.

ADDING THE SECOND FINGER

Cover the second hole with the second finger of your left hand.
You now have three holes covered . . . the thumb hole (underneath)
and the first two holes (on top). Blow gently.

This note is A.

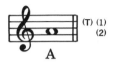

A

Play by blowing once for each note.
At the rest sign say "rest."

D7 (Autoharp)

A   A   A (rest) A   A   A (rest)

A TWO-NOTE TUNE

Here is a tune in the same rhythm, using both of the notes you have learned.

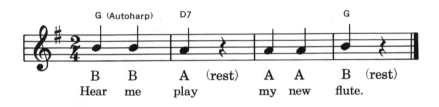

G (Autoharp)   D7   G

B   B   A   (rest)   A   A   B   (rest)
Hear me play   my new flute.

Beat as you read the plays and rests . . . Say the pitch names as you beat . . .
Play the melody . . . Be sure to say "rest" when you come to a rest sign . . . .
Now, half the class sing while the others play . . . Change parts . . .
Try singing the melody without playing.

ADDING THE THIRD FINGER

Keep your left thumb and fingers covering the thumb hole and
the first and second holes on top. Now cover the third hole
with the third finger of your left hand. Blow gently.

This note is G.

G

Play by blowing once for each note.
At the rest sign say "rest."

G (Autoharp)

G   G   G   G   G   G

117

A THREE-NOTE TUNE

Here is a longer rhythmic pattern and melody. Notice the step-bend (half) notes.
How many times would you say "play" before saying "rest"?
Read the "plays" as you beat with a big arm motion.
Can you say the pitch names as you beat?

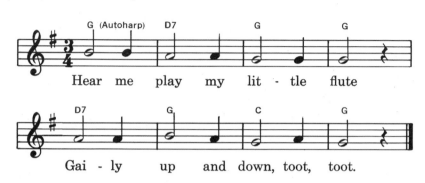

G (Autoharp)   D7   G   G

Hear   me   play   my   lit - tle   flute

D7   G   C   G

Gai - ly   up   and   down, toot, toot.

Half of the class can sing while the rest play . . . Change parts . . .
All can try singing the melody.

A NEW RHYTHM

Walk and run to the following rhythm:

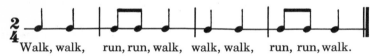

2/4
Walk, walk,   run, run, walk,   walk, walk,   run, run, walk.

BEGINNING TO USE THE RIGHT HAND

Keep your left thumb and three fingers covering the thumb hole and the
first, second, and third holes.
Now cover up the fourth hole with the first finger of your right hand. Blow gently.

This note is F.   Play the new note to this rhythm.

F   (T) (1)
                (2)
                (3)
                (4)

F (Autoharp)

COVERING THE FIFTH HOLE

Keeping your other fingers in position, place the second finger of your right hand on the fifth hole.

This note is E.

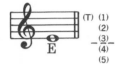

Play E to this rhythm.

COVERING THE SIXTH HOLE

Keep your other fingers in position. Place the third finger of your right hand on the sixth hole.

This note is D.

Play D to this rhythm.

COVERING ALL THE HOLES

Cover the seventh hole with the fourth finger of your right hand. Now all the holes are covered.

This note is C.

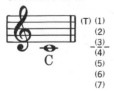

Play C.

USING OUR NEW NOTES

Walk and run to the following rhythm. Step-bend on (♩).

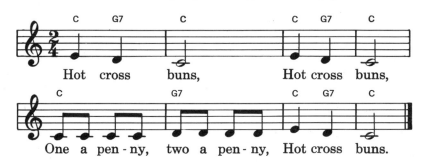

Hot cross buns, Hot cross buns,

One a pen-ny, two a pen-ny, Hot cross buns.

As you beat, read aloud the pitch names . . . Play the melody . . . Half the class sing while the rest play . . . All of the class sing.

FINISHING OUR SCALE

Take all your fingers off the top holes. Leave only the thumb hole covered.

This note is C.

Play C to this rhythm.

A SCALE SONG

Move to the rhythm of this song.

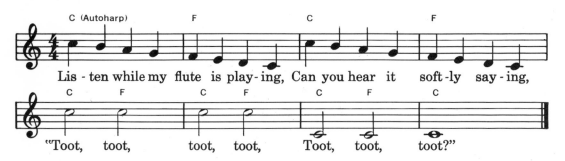

Lis-ten while my flute is play-ing, Can you hear it soft-ly say-ing,

"Toot, toot, toot, toot, Toot, toot, toot?"

Half the class sing while the rest play . . . Sing the second line while the rest of the class play the first line . . . All of the class sing.

AT THE PIANO

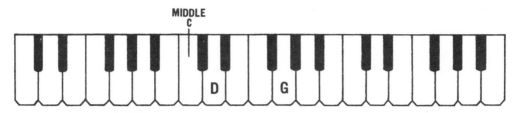

Can you find D between the two black keys nearest the middle of the piano?

How many D's can you find on the keyboard?

Try playing them with your right hand.

Now try playing them with your left hand.

Go back to the middle of the piano.

Play the D nearest the middle.

Find the G nearest to the right of D.

Play the highest G that you can find with your right hand.

Now play the lowest G with your left hand.

Play all the G's you can find, from the lowest to the highest.

Put your right pointing finger on D and your little finger on G.

Play G, D, G twice before the class sings and throughout the song.

The Farmer in the Dell

SINGING GAME

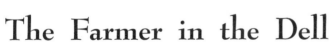

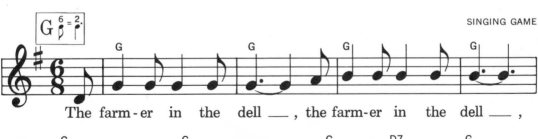

The farm-er in the dell ___, the farm-er in the dell ___,

Heigh-ho, the der-ry oh, The farm-er in the dell ___.

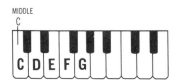

MIDDLE
C
C D E F G

For playing the piano, the fingers are numbered as in the picture above. Sing the song as you play the piece in the air with your fingers. The numbers over the notes tell you which fingers to use.

Be sure to notice where the tune moves up or down and where it moves by steps or by skips.

Find the middle of the keyboard.

Place your thumb on middle C and the other fingers on the four white keys to the right of C.

Children Running

OLD SONG

See the chil-dren run-ning, run-ning, run-ning, run-ning,

See the chil-dren run-ning 'round the room.

MIDDLE C

C E G C E G C E G

When you play these three notes together you have a chord.

Play this with your right hand as the class sings the melody below.

Now try it with your left hand as the class sings.

Sing "Row, Row, Row Your Boat" as someone plays this same chord lower on the keyboard. You might like to sing this melody as a round as someone plays this chord.

Row, Row, Row Your Boat

OLD ROUND

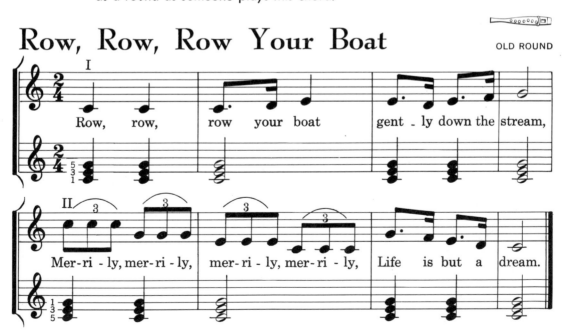

Row, row, row your boat gent - ly down the stream,

Mer-ri - ly, mer-ri - ly, mer-ri - ly, mer-ri - ly, Life is but a dream.

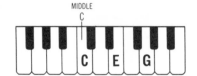 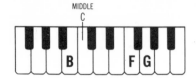

Play these chords with your right hand.

Now play the same chords with your left hand.

Notice that this melody begins with the third finger.

A-Hunting We Will Go

ENGLISH FOLK SONG

Oh, a-hunt-ing we will go, A-hunt-ing we will go,

We'll catch a fox and put him in a box and nev-er let him go.

124

JOHANN SEBASTIAN BACH
(1685–1750)

Johann Sebastian Bach was one of the most famous composers who ever lived. The music he wrote over two hundred years ago is still played and enjoyed today. He played the organ, and composed many beautiful pieces for it. He also wrote music for piano, violin, and orchestra, and music for people to sing.

Now Let Every Tongue Adore Thee

(from the cantata, "Sleepers, Wake!")

MELODY BY PHILIPP NICOLAI
ADAPTED BY JOHANN SEBASTIAN BACH

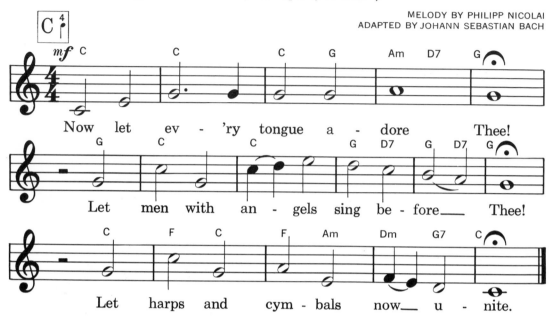

Now let ev-'ry tongue a-dore Thee!

Let men with an-gels sing be-fore___ Thee!

Let harps and cym-bals now___ u-nite.

Bach came from a very musical family. Four of his children also became famous musicians. Often the family would gather and make music together. Pretend you are part of his family as you play this minuet on your percussion instruments.

Minuet in G

JOHANN SEBASTIAN BACH

Moderately fast

126

X = Cymbals

127

FRANZ JOSEPH HAYDN
(1732–1809)

Franz Joseph Haydn was an Austrian composer. He is sometimes called Papa Haydn because some people believe that he was the father of the symphony.

On Our Way Rejoicing

MUSIC BY FRANZ JOSEPH HAYDN
WORDS BY JOHN S. MONSELL

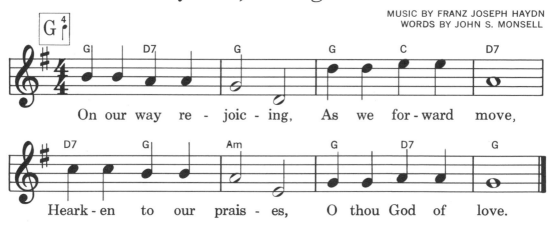

On our way re - joic - ing, As we for - ward move,

Heark - en to our prais - es, O thou God of love.

Papa Haydn loved to play jokes on people. Sometimes, when concerts were very long, people became drowsy. Some even fell asleep when the music was soft and slow. Haydn wrote a symphony to surprise these people. He called it the "Surprise Symphony."

Listen to this music and play it on your percussion instruments.

128

From the second movement of the

Surprise Symphony

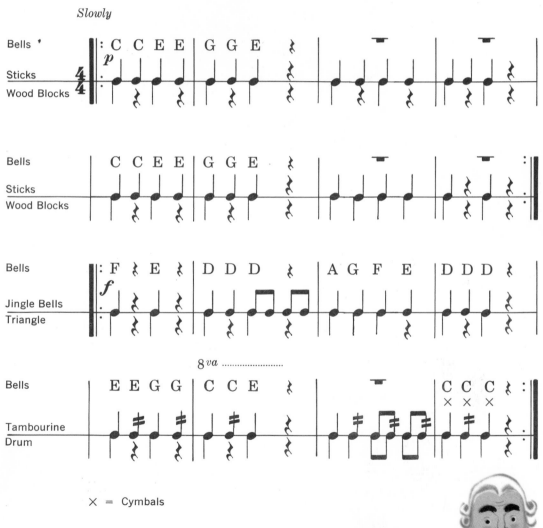

X = Cymbals

How did Haydn surprise the sleeping people?

WOLFGANG AMADEUS MOZART
(1756–1791)

Wolfgang Amadeus Mozart was another Austrian composer. He lived in Haydn's time but was much younger than Haydn.

Mozart wrote much of his music when he was no older than you. He even gave concerts with his sister when he was just six years old.

Mozart played at the courts of kings and nobles. The favorite dance of these people was a slow, stately dance called the minuet. Mozart wrote a beautiful minuet for his opera, *Don Giovanni*.

As you listen to this lovely minuet, try to picture a large ballroom with ladies in beautiful gowns dancing gracefully beside men in elegant satin suits with flowing lace cuffs.

Now play this music with your percussion instruments.

The Blacksmith

WOLFGANG AMADEUS MOZART

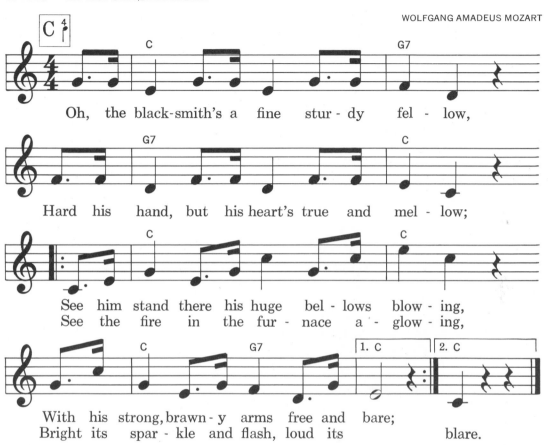

Oh, the black-smith's a fine stur-dy fel - low,

Hard his hand, but his heart's true and mel - low;

See him stand there his huge bel - lows blow - ing,
See the fire in the fur - nace a - glow - ing,

With his strong, brawn - y arms free and bare;
Bright its spar - kle and flash, loud its blare.

Minuet
(from Don Giovanni)

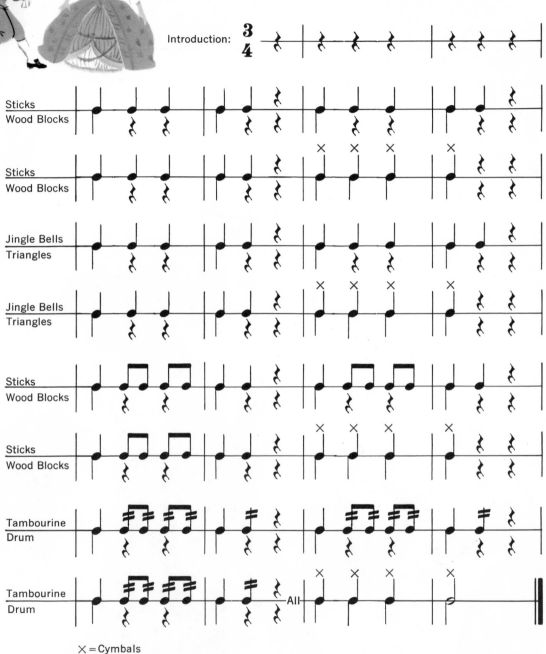

X = Cymbals

How is the minuet different from dance music of today?

Festival of the Seasons

Sing a Song of Seasons

MUSIC BY LILLY FLODDEN ANDERSON
WORDS BY ROBERT LOUIS STEVENSON

Sing a song of sea-sons, Some-thing bright in all ___,

Flow-ers in the sum-mer, Fires in the fall ___.

Autumn Fun

MUSIC AND WORDS BY ANNE KAELIN

1. Au-tumn leaves of red and gold are fall-ing through the air ___,
2. Roll-ing, slid-ing, jump-ing, hid-ing, Oh what fun to play ___

1. They make a mag-ic car-pet for chil-dren ev-'ry-where ___.
2. Up-on this mag-ic car-pet of leaves, this au-tumn day ___.

Melody Instruments

Sing { C G B F A E G
       do sol ti fa la mi sol
       8 5 7 4 6 3 5

How would you move to this music?

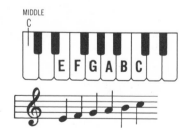

MIDDLE
C

E F G A B C

134

The Wind

MUSIC ADAPTED FROM FRED D. ALLEN
WORDS ADAPTED FROM ROBERT LOUIS STEVENSON

1. I saw you toss the kites on high,
2. I saw the dif - f'rent things you did,

1. And ___ blow the birds a - bout the sky,
2. But ___ al - ways you your - self you hid,

1. And all a - round I hear you pass,
2. I felt you push, I heard you call,

1. While ___ blow - ing all the blades of grass.
2. I ___ could not see your - self at all.

Refrain

O wind, a - blow - ing all day long!

O wind, that sings so loud a song!

135

Trick or Treat

MUSIC AND WORDS BY ANNE KAELIN

1. Witch - es, ghosts, and gob - lins Steal - ing down the street,
2. When your door is o - pened, This is what you meet,

1. Knock on ev - 'ry door - way, TRICK OR TREAT!
2. Scar - y crea - tures shout - ing, TRICK OR TREAT!

136

The Ghost of Tom

SOURCE UNKNOWN

Have you seen the ghost of Tom?

Eyes bugged out and＿ nose too long＿,

With＿ big ug - ly teeth and a shin - y white chin,

On - ly one cheek to keep his tongue in.

137

Halloween Is Very Queer

MUSIC BY GEORGE H. SHAPIRO
WORDS BY GLADYS L. ADSHEAD

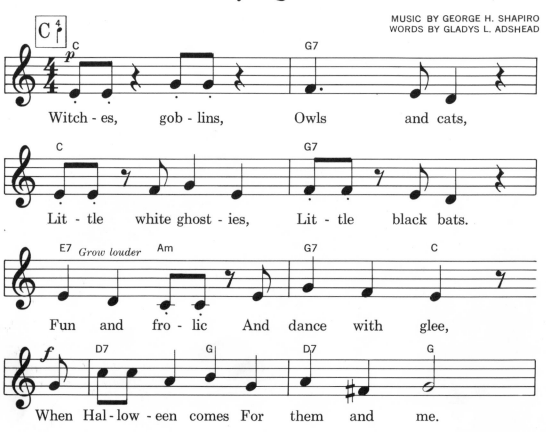

Witch - es, gob - lins, Owls and cats,

Lit - tle white ghost - ies, Lit - tle black bats.

Fun and fro - lic And dance with glee,

When Hal - low - een comes For them and me.

"Boo!" says the witch, "Boo to you!"

"Boo!" says the gob-lin and the ghost - ie, too.

Faster

Boo! Boo! Boo! Boo! Boo! Hal - low - een is

here When eve - ry - thing is ver - y queer! Boo!

∥ is a sign that tells us to pause for a moment. Can you find it in the song?
If you look carefully you will find other signs. Do you know what they mean?

The First Thanksgiving

MUSIC BY FREDERICH C. MAKER
WORDS BY DORIS R. FISHER

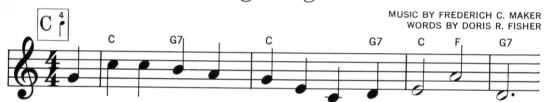

1. When pil-grims came to Ply-mouth town so long a - go
2. When spring ar - rived and flow - ers bloomed, new hope was born;

1. To find a land where free-dom's light for them would glow;
2. They gath-ered 'round to till the ground and plant the corn;

1. They suf-fered through the win-ter's freez - ing cold and snow.
2. And har - vest days brought songs of praise to greet each morn.

3. With grateful hearts they then declared a holiday
   For feasting and rejoicing, to give thanks and pray;
   And so, to us they gave the first Thanksgiving Day.

Song of Thanks

MUSIC AND WORDS BY ALBERTO RANDEGGER

1. Birds and bees and flow - ers, Ev - 'ry hap - py day___ ,
2. So the lit - tle chil - dren Sleep - ing all the night___ ,

1. Wake to greet___ the sun - light, Thank - ful for its ray___ ;
2. Wake with each___ new morn - ing, Fresh and sweet and bright___ ,

1. All the night___ they're si - lent, Sleep - ing safe___ and warm___ ;
2. Thank - ing God___, their Fa - ther, For His lov - ing care ___ ;

1. God Who knows and loves them Keeps them safe from harm___ .
2. With their songs and prais - es, Mak - ing day more fair___ .

Some might like to play this on melody instruments while others sing.

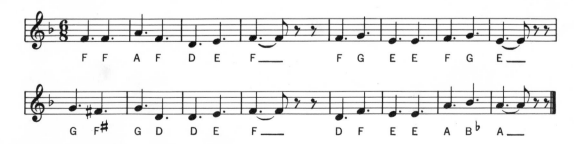

F F A F D E F___ F G E E F G E___

G F♯ G D D E F___ D F E E A B♭ A___

141

Christmas Bells Are Ringing

MUSIC BY LILLY FLODDEN ANDERSON
WORDS BY RUBYE PATTON NORDGREN

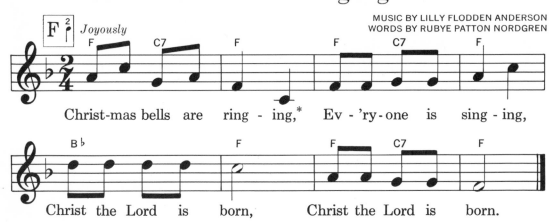

Christ-mas bells are ring-ing,* Ev-'ry-one is sing-ing,

Christ the Lord is born, Christ the Lord is born.

Play this on Melody Bells or Small Winds as an introduction.

*"Easter Bells are ringing" and "Christ the Lord is risen" may be sung instead.

142

Christmas Song

FOLK TUNE FROM SWEDEN
WORDS BY GLADYS PITCHER

1. A gen-tle Babe lay sleep-ing up-on a man-ger bare,
2. There came un-to the man-ger some shep-herds from a-far,

1. With lov-ing Ma-ry watch-ing, and Jo-seph, too, stood there;
2. And wise men came to wor-ship, came fol-low-ing a star,

1. The crea-tures all kept si-lent to see the Child so fair.
2. And wise men came to wor-ship, came fol-low-ing a star.

3. Now let us all be grateful, and worship as we may,
For God has sent a Baby, to guide us on our way,
For God has sent a Baby, to guide us on our way.

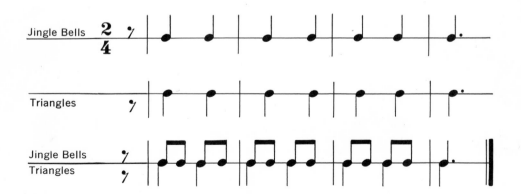

Jingle Bells

Triangles

Jingle Bells
Triangles

143

Silent Night

MUSIC BY FRANZ GRÜBER
WORDS BY JOSEPH MOHR

1. Si - lent night, Ho - ly night, All is calm, all is bright
2. Si - lent night, Ho - ly night, Shep-herds quake at the sight!

1. Round yon Vir - gin Moth - er and Child,
2. Glo - ries stream from Heav - en a - far,

1. Ho - ly In-fant, so ten - der and mild,
2. Heav'n-ly hosts sing Al - le - lu - ia,

1. Sleep in heav - en - ly peace___ , Sleep___ in heav - en - ly peace___ .
2. Christ, the Sav - ior, is born___ , Christ___, the Sav - ior, is born___ .

Some might like to play the rhythm ‖: ♩ ♪ ♪ ♩. :‖ on resonator
bells or Swiss bells while others sing the song.

    Group I play C chord (C E G)

    Group II play G7 chord (G B D F)

    Group III play F chord (F A C)

144

Long Ago in Bethlehem

MUSIC BY EDITH PLATT
WORDS BY HAZEL S. NEAL

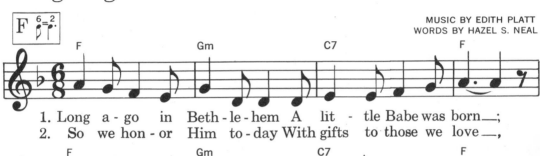

1. Long a-go in Beth-le-hem A lit-tle Babe was born—;
2. So we hon-or Him to-day With gifts to those we love—,

1. All the heav'n-ly an-gels sang On that first Christ-mas morn—.
2. Thank-ful for our bless-ings great That come from God a-bove—.

Refrain

Shep-herds knelt be-fore Him, awed. Wise men came from far—;

Gifts they brought and wor-shiped Him, Led by one bright star—.

145

We Wish You a Merry Christmas

TRADITIONAL

1. We wish you a mer-ry Christ-mas, we wish you a mer-ry Christ-mas,
2. Oh bring us some fig-gy pud-ding, Oh bring us some fig-gy pud-ding,

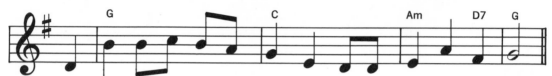

1. We wish you a mer-ry Christ-mas, and a hap-py New Year!
2. Oh bring us some fig-gy pud-ding, please __ bring it out here!

Refrain

We wish you joy, we wish you good cheer,

We wish you a mer-ry Christ-mas, and a hap-py New Year!

146

The Lights of Hanukkah

(Chanuko)

MUSIC AND WORDS
BY RAY N. COOK

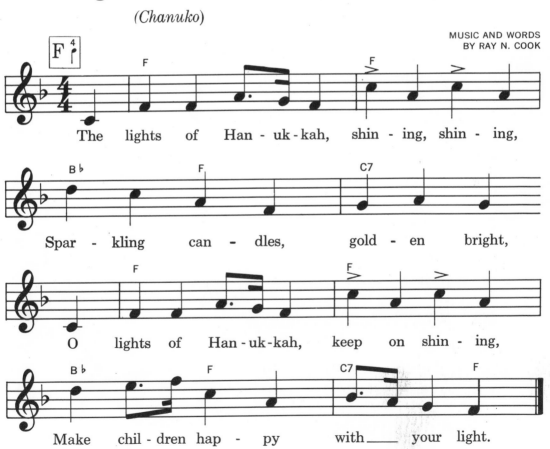

The lights of Han-uk-kah, shin-ing, shin-ing,

Spar-kling can-dles, gold-en bright,

O lights of Han-uk-kah, keep on shin-ing,

Make chil-dren hap-py with___ your light.

Skating

MUSIC BY EMIL WALDTEUFEL
WORDS ADAPTED

1. Win - ter is here_____ , best time of year_____ ;
2. Win - ter is here_____ , best time of year_____ ;

1. Come on a - long, sing a skat - ing song_____ .
2. Skat - ing and sing - ing we glide a - long_____ .

1&2. First on the ice we go slip - ping and slid - ing

1&2. And then in a trice we are grace - ful - ly glid - ing.

1&2. Now slip - ping and slid - ing or grace - ful - ly glid - ing

1&2. We'll sing a - long _____ .

Pretend you are ice skating.

Skating

(Percussion Score)

Valentine Hearts

W. R. F.
D. R. F.

Hearts of pa - per, Hearts of lace,

Wher - ev - er I look I see hearts ev - 'ry place.

On this one I've writ - ten, "O will you be mine?"

I want you to be my Val - en - tine.

Greetings of Spring
(Frühlingsgruss)

MUSIC BY MENDELSSOHN
WORDS BY H. HEINE
ENGLISH ADAPTATION BY DORIS FISHER

1. Soft - ly sound-ing in my heart Dis-tant bells are ring - ing;
GERMAN: *Lei - se zieht durch mein Ge - müt lieb - li - ches Ge - l'au - te;*

Sing your lit - tle song of spring, Na-ture's mes-sage bring - ing.
Klin - ge, klei - nes Früh-lings-lied, kling' hin-aus ins Wei - te.

2. Sing it where the violet grows, Softly keep repeating;
   (*Kling' hinaus bis an das Haus, Wo die Veilchen spriessen;*)
   Then, if you should see a rose, Bring it spring's first greeting.
   (*Wenn du eine Rose schaust, Sag' ich lass' sie grüssen.*)

151

Bell Carol

FRENCH TUNE
WORDS BY W. R. F.

From ev'ry stee-ple ring the joy-ous Eas-ter bells, And
ev'ry ring-ing bell a hap-py mes-sage tells;

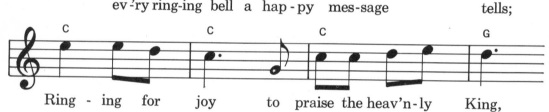

Ring - ing for joy to praise the heav'n-ly King,

And call all men of faith_____ To praise the Lord and sing.

You may play this descant on bells as the class sings the song.

A E A E B E E A

C E E G E A D E A

Adir Hu
(Song of Passover)

HEBREW SONG

Slowly

God of might, God of right, Thee we give all___ glo-ry.
HEBREW: A - dir hu, A - dir hu, Yiv - ne ve - so ___ b'ko - rov.

Thine all praise___ in these days As in a - ges hoar - y.
Bim - hey - ro ___, Bim - hey - ro, B'yo - mey nu b' - ko - rov.

When we hear, year by year, Free-dom's won-drous sto - ry.
El b' - ney, El b' - ney, B'nay ves - ho b' - ko - rov.

The Holiday

OLD DUTCH SONG

1. What shall we do when____ we go out, we go out, we go out,
2. We will____ take a____ horse to ride, horse to ride, horse to ride,

1. What shall we do when____ we go out on our hol - i - day?
2. We will____ take a____ horse to ride on our hol - i - day.

What else could we do on our holiday?

Friendship

MUSIC BY LUDWIG VAN BEETHOVEN
AUTHOR UNKNOWN

1. Love is to hu-man hearts   What sun-shine is to flow'rs,
2. If we should walk a - lone,   We learn in lone-ly hours

1. And friend-ship is the   fair-est thing In this great world of ours.
2. That friend-ship is the   fair-est thing In this great world of ours.

Birthday Song

W. R. F.
D. R. F.

Close your eyes,   make a wish,   I hope your wish comes true;

A ver - y hap - py birth-day   I wish for   you.

If You're Happy

F 4/4 *Gaily*

F   C7

1. If you're hap-py and you know it, clap your hands, (CLAP,   CLAP)

C7   F

If you're hap-py and you know it, clap your hands, (CLAP,   CLAP)

B♭   F

If you're hap-py and you know it, Then your face will sure-ly show it,

C7   F

If you're hap-py and you know it, clap your hands. (CLAP,   CLAP)

2. . . . tap your toe,   (TAP, TAP)   Quarter note ♩

3. . . . nod your head, (NOD, NOD)   Quarter rest 𝄽

4. . . . do all three,   (TOGETHER)   How many rests (stop signs) can you find?

Mein Hands

PENNSYLVANIA DUTCH FOLK SONG

1-13. Mein hands by mein sides, was ist das hier?
(Hands at sides)

1. Das ist mein Hair mop - per } mein teach - er dear.
2. Das ist mein Think - box - er }
(Point to 1. hair, 2. head)

1. Hair mop - per,
2. { Think box - er }
     { Hair mop - per, }   du - ven - ick - a   von   du,

1-13. Dat's what we learn in der Schul_____ .
(Fold hands)

3. Eye blinker   6. Chin chopper   9. Bread basket
4. Smell sniffer   7. Rubber necker   10. Lap sitter
5. Soup sipper   8. Chest protector   11. Knee bender
12. Road runner   13. Flat footer

157

All Things Bright and Beautiful

MUSIC BY WILLIAM H. MONK
WORDS BY CECIL F. ALEXANDER

1. All things bright and beau - ti - ful, All crea-tures great and small,
2. He gave us two eyes to see, And lips that we might tell,

1. All things wise and won - der - ful, The Lord God made them all.
2. Great is God Al - might - y, Who has made all things well.

All Night, All Day

SPIRITUAL

Refrain

1&2. All night, all ____ day,

1&2. An - gels watch-in' o - ver me, my Lord ____ .

1&2. All night, all day,

1&2. An - gels watch - in' o - ver me _____ . *Fine* *End*

Verse
1. Now I lay me down to sleep,
2. If I die be - fore I wake,

1. An - gels watch - in' o - ver me, my Lord ___ .
2. An - gels watch - in' o - ver me, my Lord ___ .

1. Pray the Lord my soul ___ to keep,
2. Pray the Lord my soul ___ to take,

1. An - gels watch - in' o - ver me _____ . *D.C.*
2. An - gels watch - in' o - ver me _____ . *Go to the beginning*

America

MUSIC ATTRIBUTED TO HENRY CAREY
WORDS BY SAMUEL FRANCIS SMITH

1. My coun-try, 'tis of thee,
2. My na-tive coun-try, thee,

1. Sweet land of lib-er-ty, Of thee I sing;
2. Land of the no-ble free, Thy name I love;

1. Land where my fa-thers died, Land of the Pil-grims' pride,
2. I love thy rocks and rills, Thy woods and tem-pled hills;

1. From ev-'ry_ moun-tain side, Let_ free-dom ring!
2. My heart_with_ rap-ture thrills, Like_that a-bove.

3. Our fathers' God, to Thee, Author of liberty,
   To Thee we sing.
   Long may our land be bright, With freedom's holy light;
   Protect us by Thy might, Great God our King!

160

For Health and Strength

TRADITIONAL ROUND

I
For health and strength and dai - ly food,

II
We praise Thy name, O Lord.

Fifty Stars

MUSIC BY WILLIAM R. FISHER
WORDS BY DORIS R. FISHER

1. There are fif - ty stars in our flag, Up - on a field of blue;
2. There are fif - ty states in our land, A star for each 'tis true;

1&2. I love the fif - ty stars — In the red, white and blue.

161

America, the Beautiful

MUSIC BY SAMUEL A. WARD
WORDS BY KATHERINE LEE BATES

1. O beau-ti-ful for spa-cious skies, For am-ber waves of grain.
2. O beau-ti-ful for pa-triot dream That sees be-yond the years,

1. For pur-ple moun-tain maj-es-ties A-bove the fruit-ed plain!
2. Thine al-a-bas-ter cit-ies gleam Un-dimmed by hu-man tears!

1&2. A-mer-i-ca! A-mer-i-ca! God shed His grace on thee,

1&2. And crown thy good with broth-er-hood, From sea to shin-ing sea!

162

CLASSIFIED INDEX

164

ALPHABETICAL INDEX

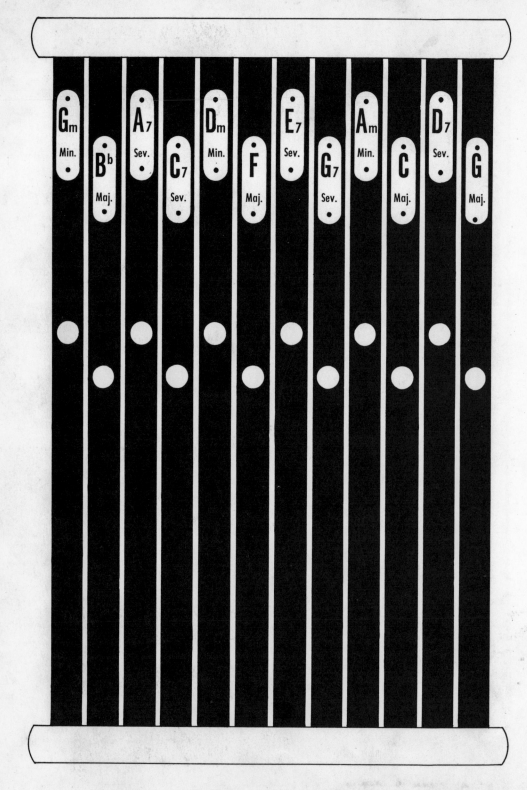